Perspective Globs

36 PHOTOS & 36 THOUGHTS

STARRY TENT

Copyright © 2022 STARRY TENT

All rights reserved.

No part of this publication may be reproduced or transmitted in any form or by any means, electronic or mechanical, including photocopying, recording, or by any information storage and retrieval system, without written permission of the publisher.

ISBN: 9798407760054
Imprint: Independently published

For Michelle, Rebecca & Lydia oh Lydia ~

a Lionheart,
a Queen,
&
a True Sage

CONTENTS

Photo 1:	Sun Sets, Burning	Pg 1
Photo 2:	The Well	Pg 3
Photo 3:	A Horse's Freedom	Pg 5
Photo 4:	Butterfly Blue	Pg 7
Photo 5:	Spring Haiku	Pg 9
Photo 6:	The Wisdom of Cats	Pg 11
Photo 7:	Bliss, Do Not Fade	Pg 13
Photo 8:	An Easter Miracle	Pg 15
Photo 9:	Lives & Leaves	Pg 17
Photo 10:	The Secret of Flowers	Pg 19
Photo 11:	The Stone Bride	Pg 21
Photo 12:	Horizon Speaks	Pg 23
Photo 13:	Summer Haiku	Pg 25
Photo 14:	A Cry of a Dragonfly	Pg 27
Photo 15:	From Sole to Deep	Pg 29
Photo 16:	Umma	Pg 31
Photo 17:	Friends Forever	Pg 33
Photo 18:	Infinite Peace	Pg 35

Photo 19:	Sweet Presence	Pg 37
Photo 20:	Iliad & Beautyberry	Pg 39
Photo 21:	Autumn Haiku	Pg 41
Photo 22:	Mutual Healing	Pg 43
Photo 23:	Shooting Stars	Pg 45
Photo 24:	Swing Low	Pg 47
Photo 25:	Nostalgia	Pg 49
Photo 26:	Grandpa Kuho	Pg 51
Photo 27:	Stately Standing	Pg 53
Photo 28:	Pepper Harvest	Pg 55
Photo 29:	Winter Haiku	Pg 57
Photo 30:	Fireworks	Pg 59
Photo 31:	True Satisfaction	Pg 61
Photo 32:	That Wildish Streak	Pg 63
Photo 33:	Where Victory Lies	Pg 65
Photo 34:	Daisy, Daisy	Pg 67
Photo 35:	More Than a Conqueror	Pg 69
Photo 36:	Solid Friends	Pg 71
	About the Author	Pg 74

PREFACE
36 photos and 36 thoughts...

I pulled them out from various shambles of my life - Instagram posts, old emails and forgotten, shriveled up notes. Essays, poems and memoirs glumly stared at me.

In some ways, they were like shattered pieces of a porcelain pot, and I sadly laughed at the brokenness of my life.

But gradually, they started to take form. There were matching shapes, fitting colors, lost and found items... Then to my surprise, these little globs bravely hurled themselves under the mighty rolling pin called "Who Cares?" and got themselves baked into a pie - a solid lump of a book!

It is said that life is all about perspective. I hope these candid thoughts I share with you will give you something new to think about.

And since it is January, I sincerely wish you a wonderful year of 2022! May there be flowers, pastries, and good people in unexpected places.

Happy New Year, Solar & Lunar!

SUN SETS, BURNING

In the wide steppes of Mongolia, I have found many wondrous words. There is the word "Mandakh" - meaning sunrise. But it is the opposite word "Jargakh" - sunset, that fascinates me.

For the word could also mean blissfulness.

Dare I believe that the bitter past and the departed dreams could somehow, in some way, be birthing some new - perhaps some sort of happiness this very moment - in a place called my future?

Alea iacta est. The die is cast!

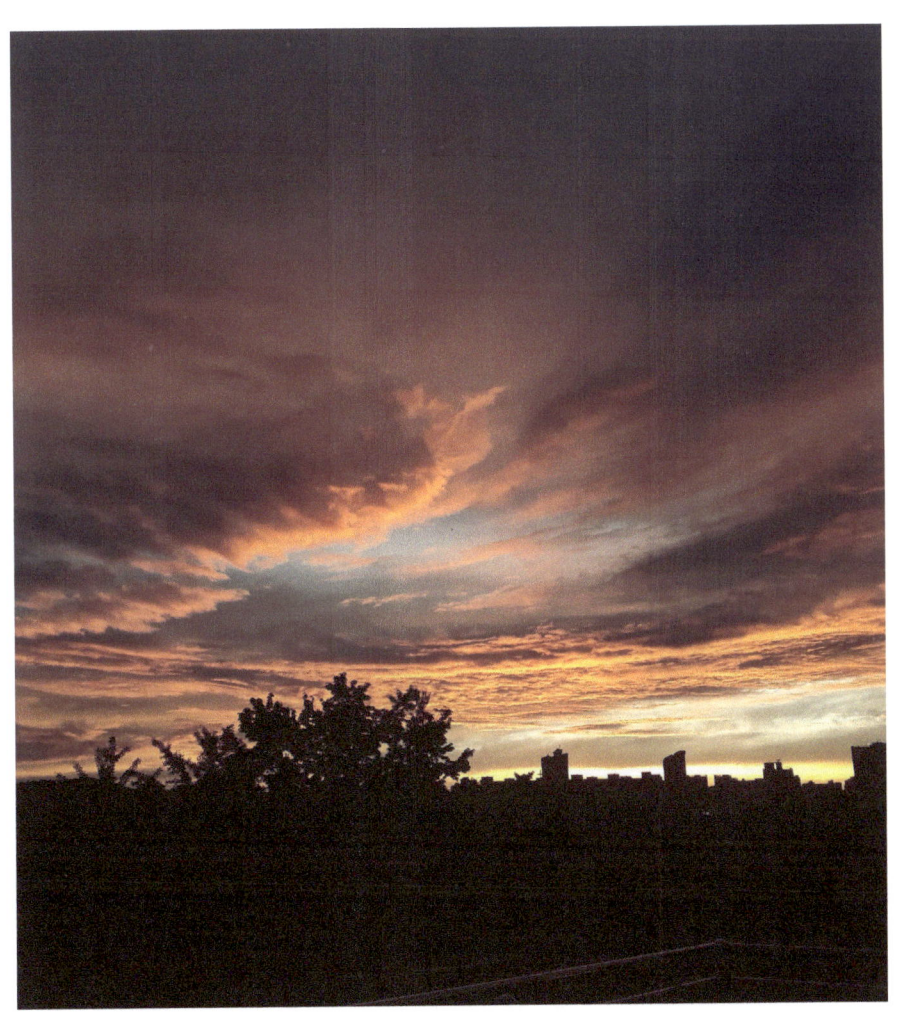

SUN SETS, BURNING.
IT MUST, TO BRING FORTH SOMETHING NEW.

THE WELL

It sat in the old church yard, untouched, unbothered, just savoring memories of serving fresh water.

Years ago, it would have quenched the thirst of the pastor and his flock. The hearty congregation buttering him up, calling the water celestially refreshing and all that sort of nonsense might still be echoing in its ears.

Now it just sits, content.

Sits and basks in the sunlight, then watches the sun set for the thousandth time.

Its labor has ended, yet its purpose remains.

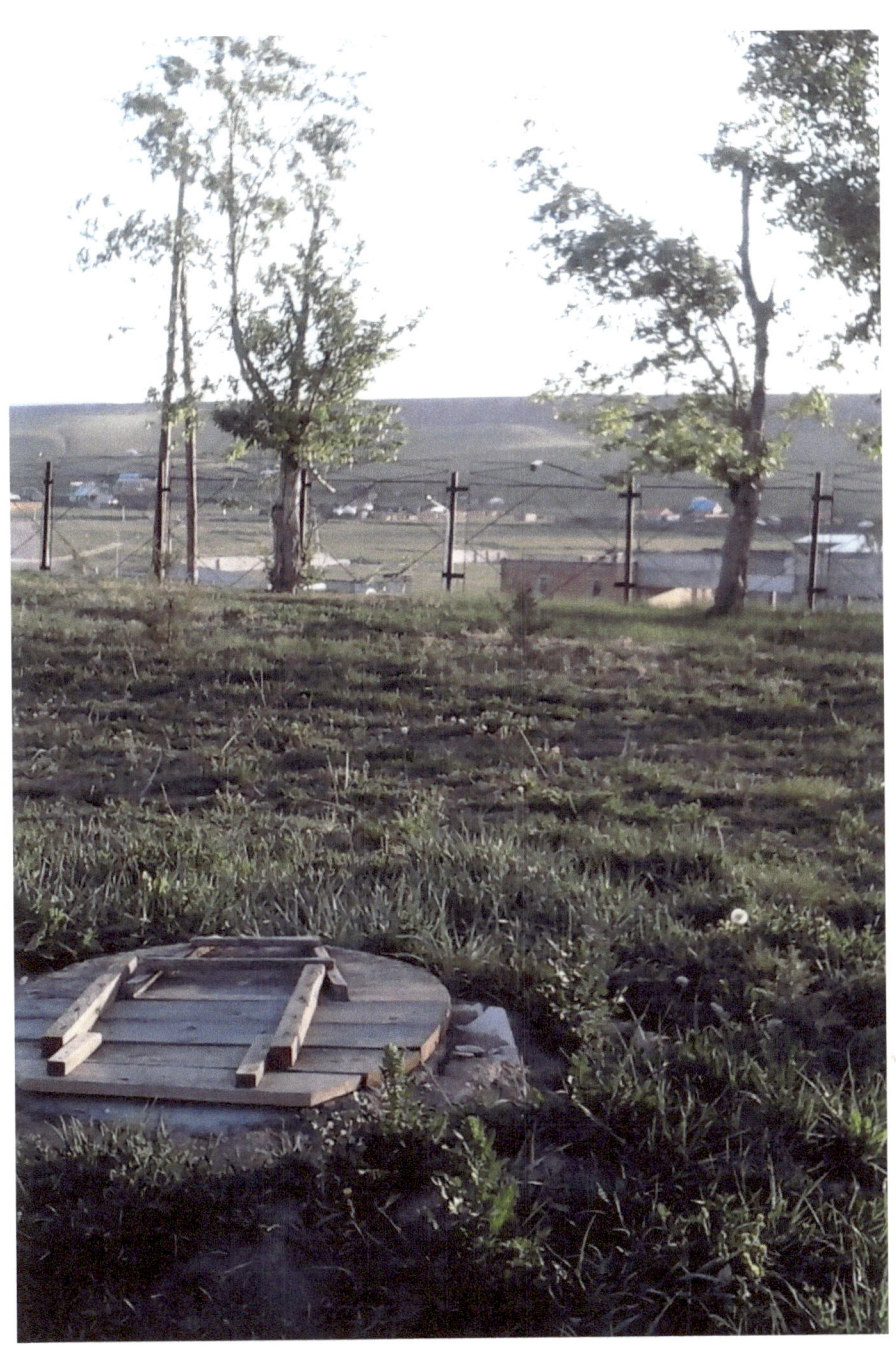

THE WELL STAYED LIKE A SCAR, CRUDE BUT CONTENT.

A HORSE'S FREEDOM

The horse rancher was branding the yearlings and my friend and I got invited to the party. We ran like the wind in the steppes, wild and shrieking unintelligent idioms to help gather the herd. Unfortunately, the horses were a bit faster than us, so the jeep drivers got to work.

Finally, the yearlings were captured, looking windblown and happy. They had a good time. Galloping and enjoying their freedom - the freedom of the unbranded.

The moment when the heated metal seared thru the flesh, I saw fear and shock come into their gentle eyes. Then relief and courage flowed back as they were once again set free to pounce on the dust with sturdy hooves.

Yet now, something was different. Already, the brand was maturing them to another level. The same freedom was theirs, only with consequences.

Snort. So what? To live they shall gallop and to gallop they shall live. The branded ones thundered away, gloriously tossing their manes to the roaring wind.

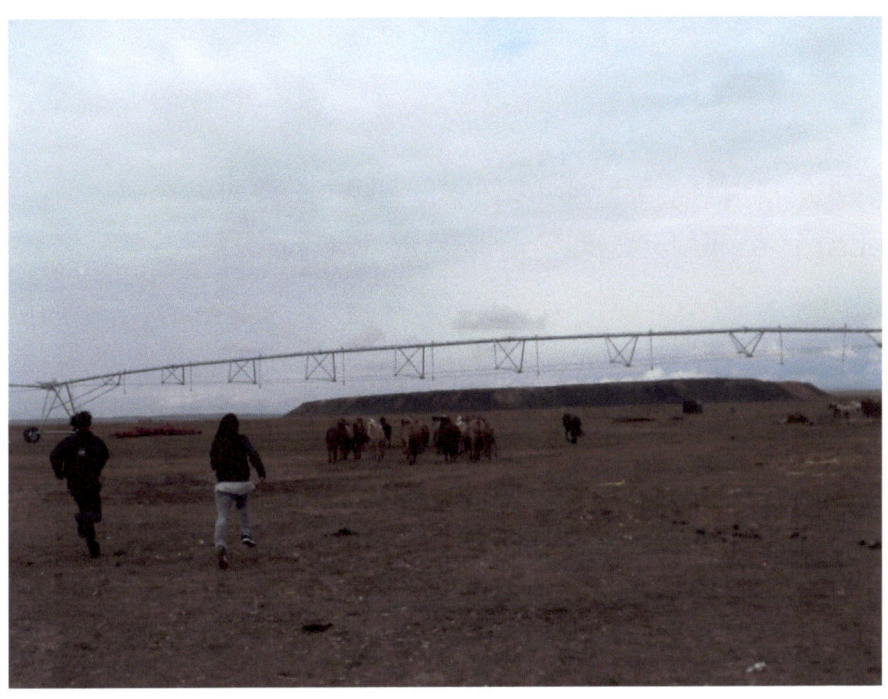

IT WAS TIME TO CHASE SOME HORSES.

BUTTERFLY BLUE

Hailed as a national flower of Mongolia, the scabiosa is a stunning flower with bitter etymology.

Named "Ber tsetseg" meaning a widow flower, it smiles serenely over the insane realities of life.

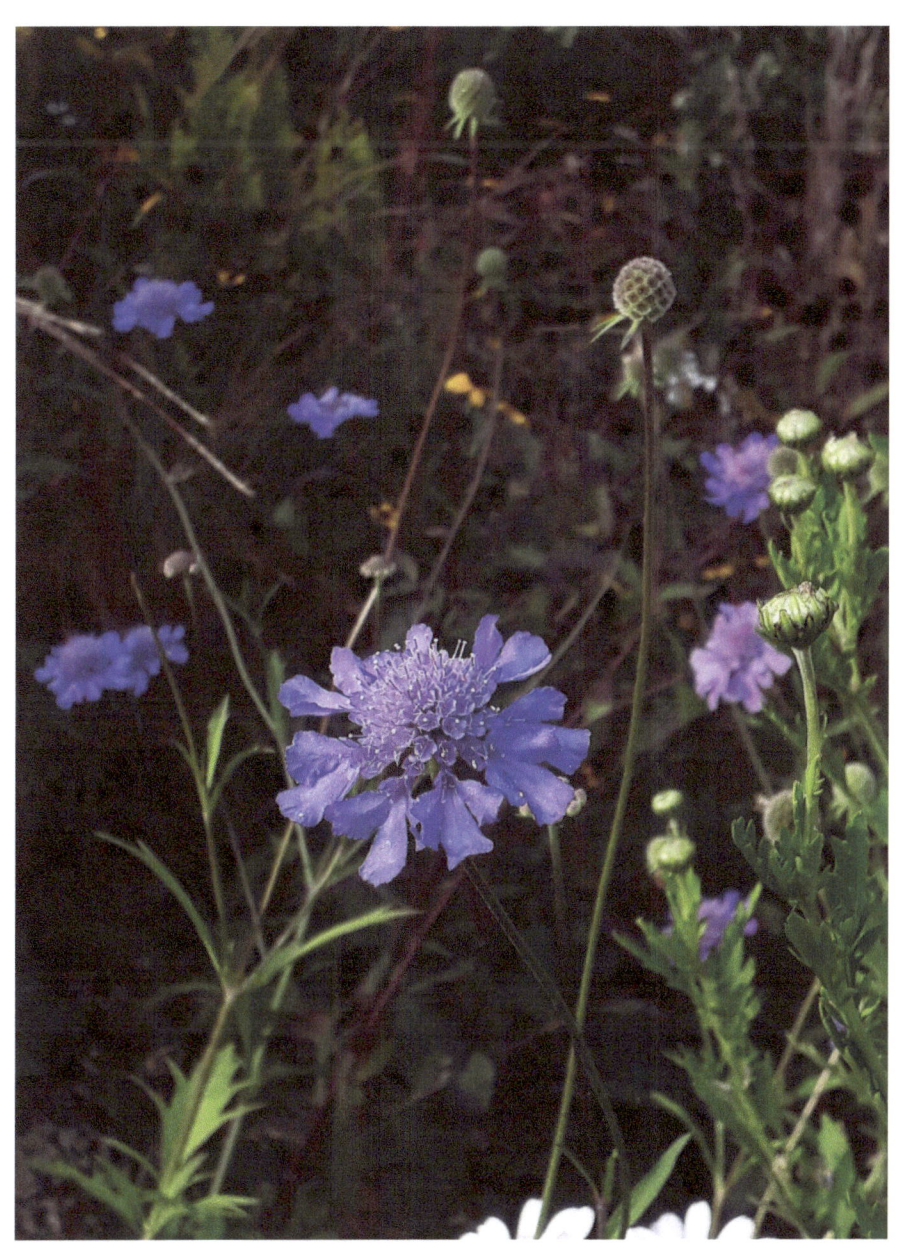

A STAUNCH LITTLE SCABIOSA.

SPRING HAIKU

You are gold, but I -
I'm just a teardrop falling
Into your splendor

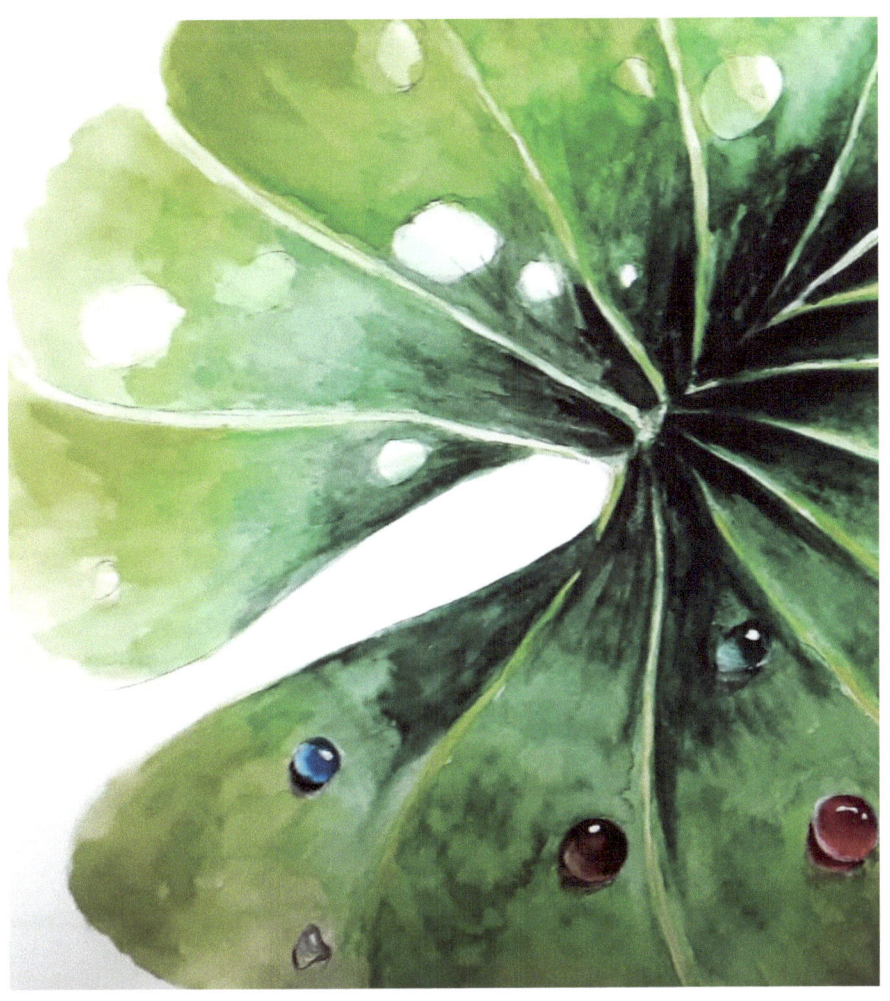

THE DEWDROP WILL RETURN WITH THE DAWN.

THE WISDOM OF CATS

What can these scowling creatures teach us?

How to find the best spot?

To bask in the sun once in a daring while?

Or just simply ignore the others
and do what you truly love to do?

Oh, to be like cats!

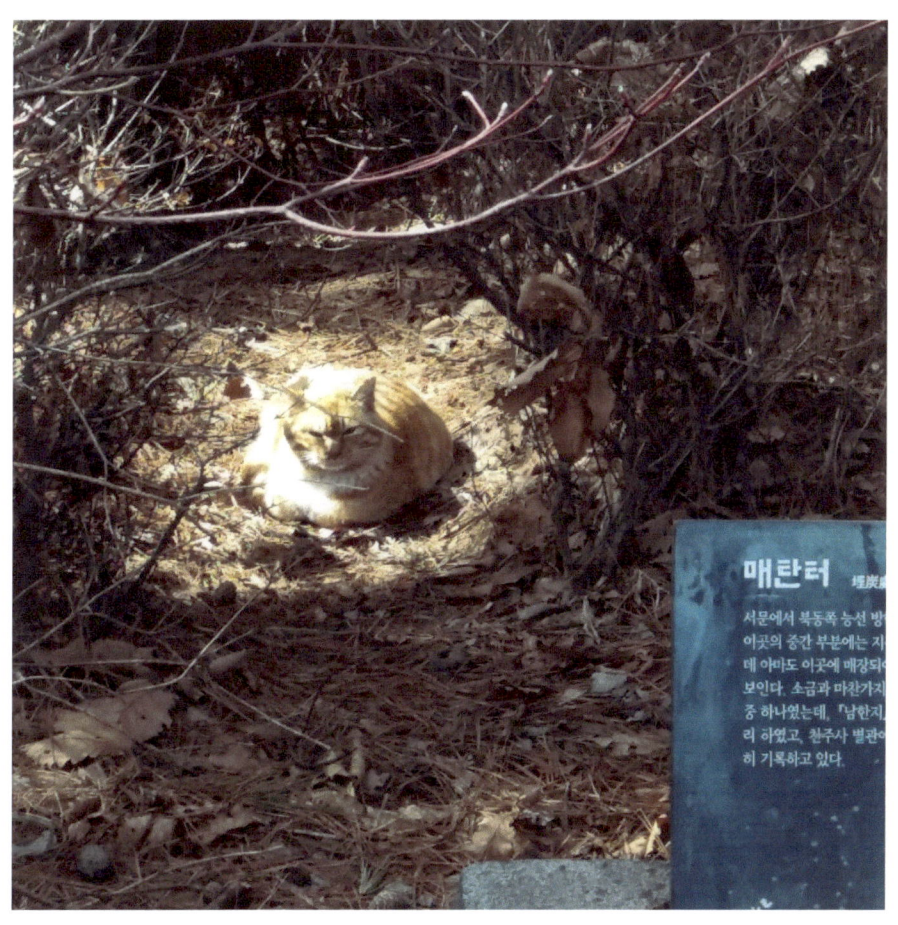

IT SAT AND SCOWLED PROFOUNDLY.

BLISS, DO NOT FADE

Paint the air with invisible fingers,

then paint them into your memories visible –

Cherry, Cherry, my sweet youth!

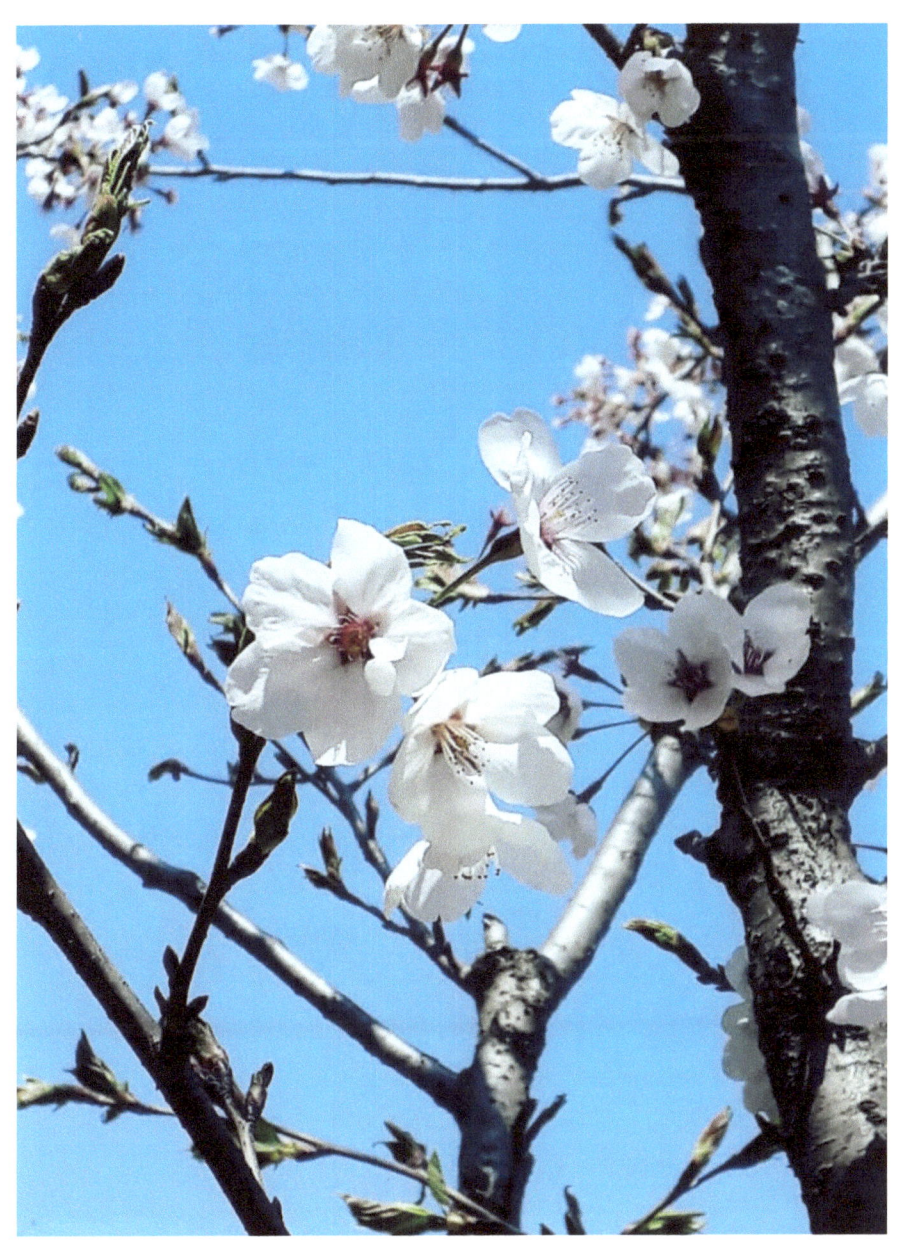

SNOWFLAKES AND STARS, WONDERS ASUNDER!

AN EASTER MIRACLE

Against all odds, my dear little Blossom had her first flower. And that on the very morning of Easter Sunday: April 21st, 2019.

She never blossomed again and has now vanished without trace – pot and all.

I think she was raptured.

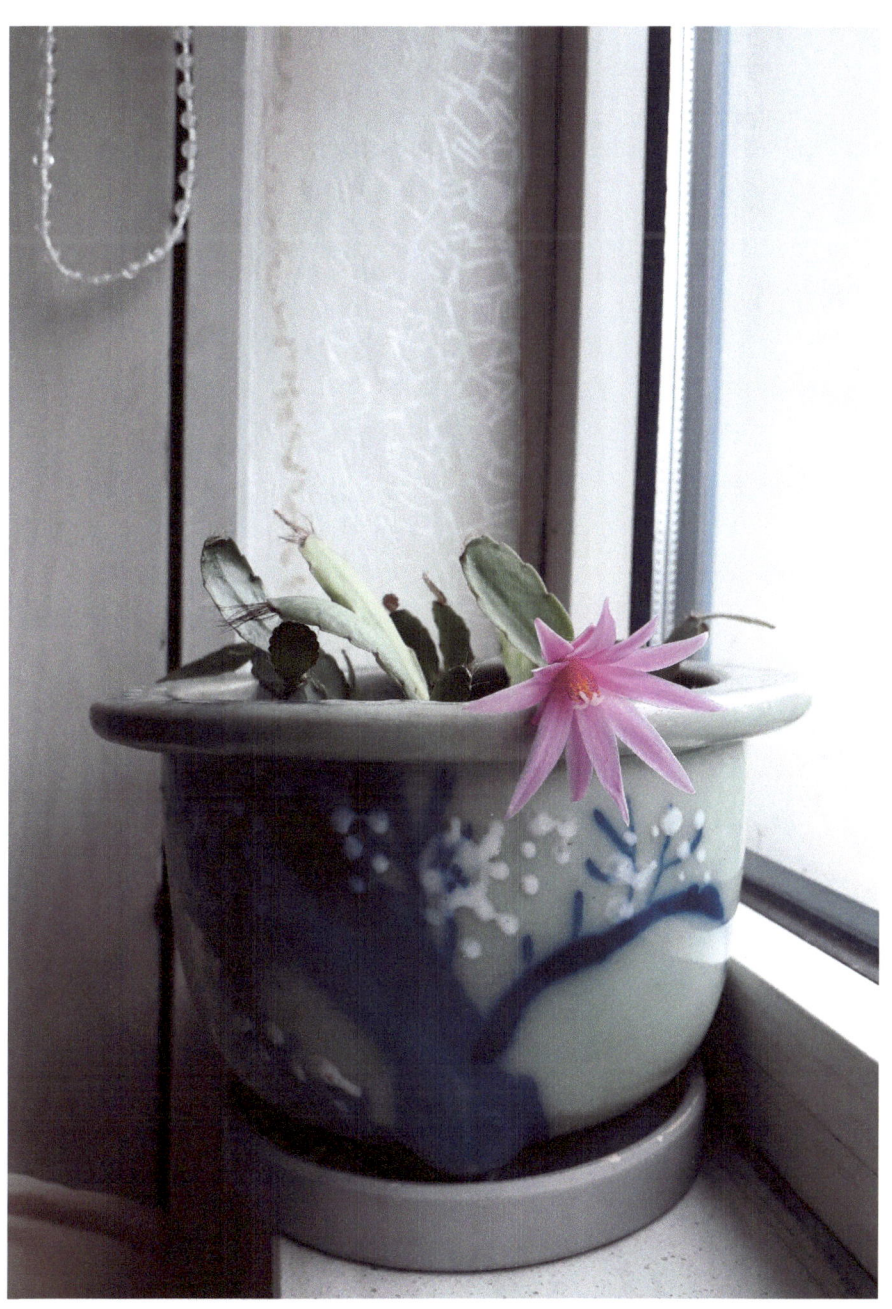

A CHRISTMAS CACTUS. THE PORCELAIN POT WAS PASSED DOWN FROM MY GREAT-GRANDMOTHER.

LIVES & LEAVES

Your story is unique.
Your triumphs, your failures, joys and losses.

Look up.

If you and I were one of those leaves,
Perhaps we could hug the branches tight
And let the life-giving sap seep into our souls.

It is time to reconnect.
It is time to live.

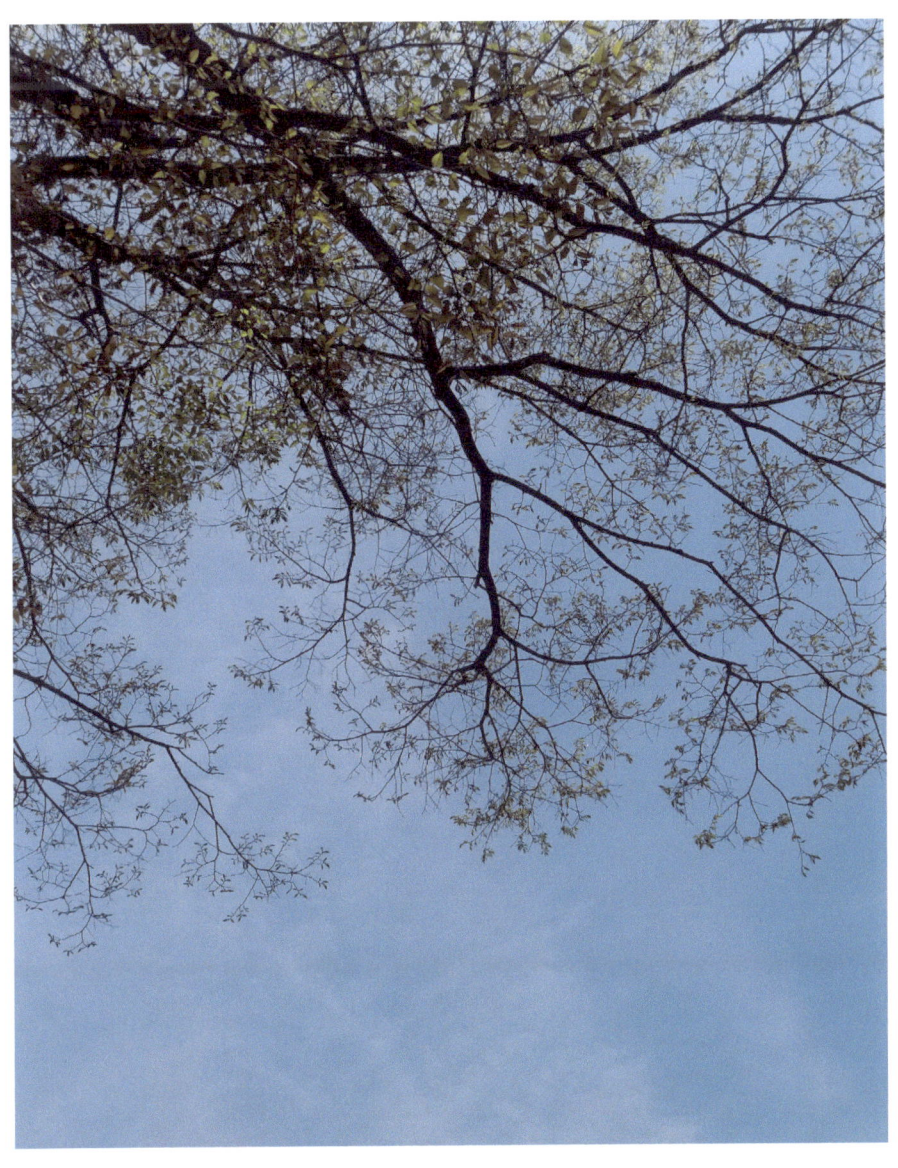

THOUSANDS OF STORIES PERCHED ABOVE.
CREATOR LOOKS THROUGH THEM ALL.

THE SECRET OF FLOWERS

The sweetness, the fragrance,
The secret of the graceful posture
May lie in their language -
The language of patience.

That's how a flower gets along with the wind.
Flowers, flowers, flowers galore!

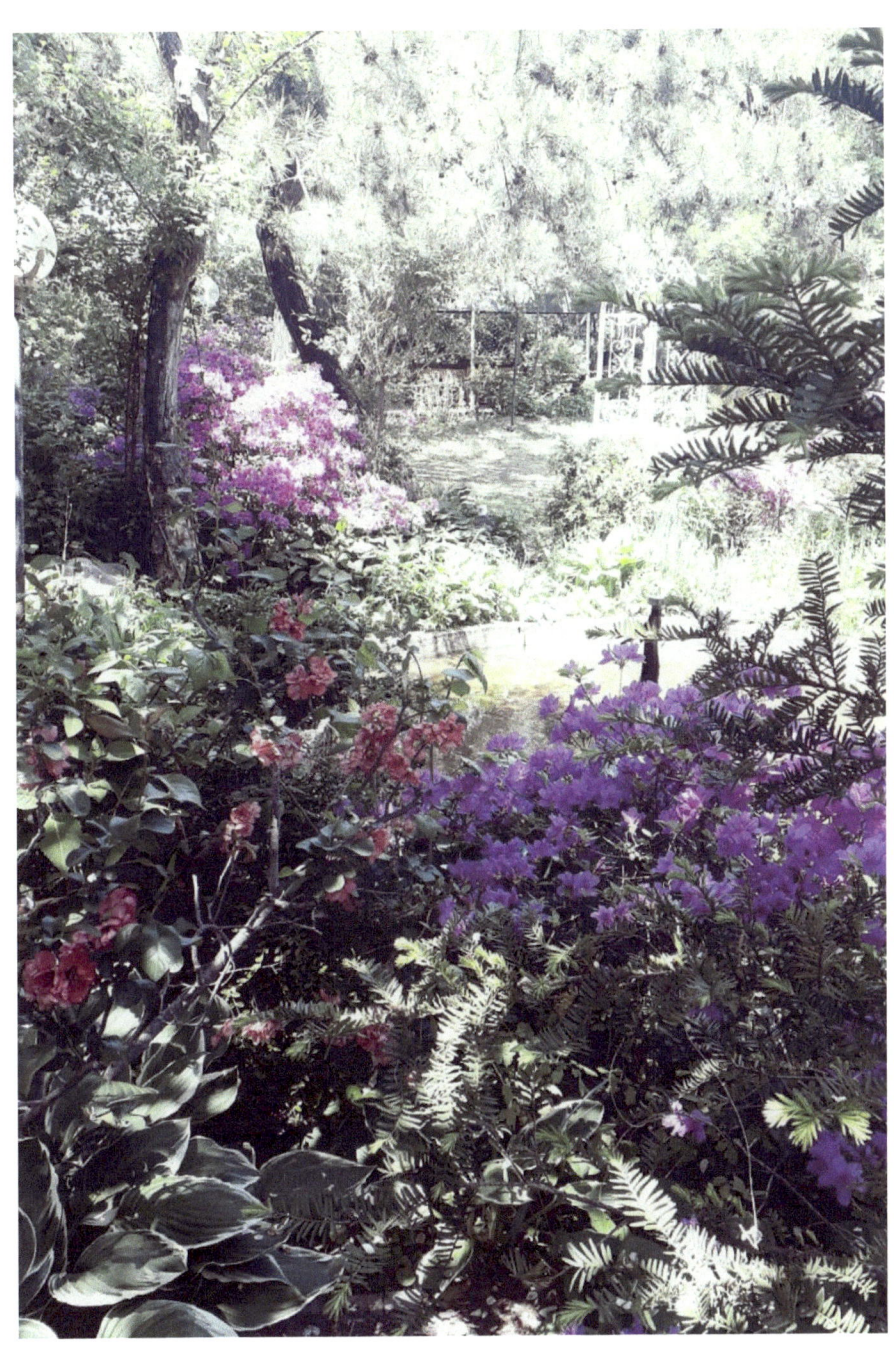

BE STILL AND LET THE WIND SPREAD YOUR SCENT.

THE STONE BRIDE

A stone bride?
You are but a cold pile of stones!

True, true – she blushes deep.
Then lets the flowers love on her –

Shower after shower after shower.

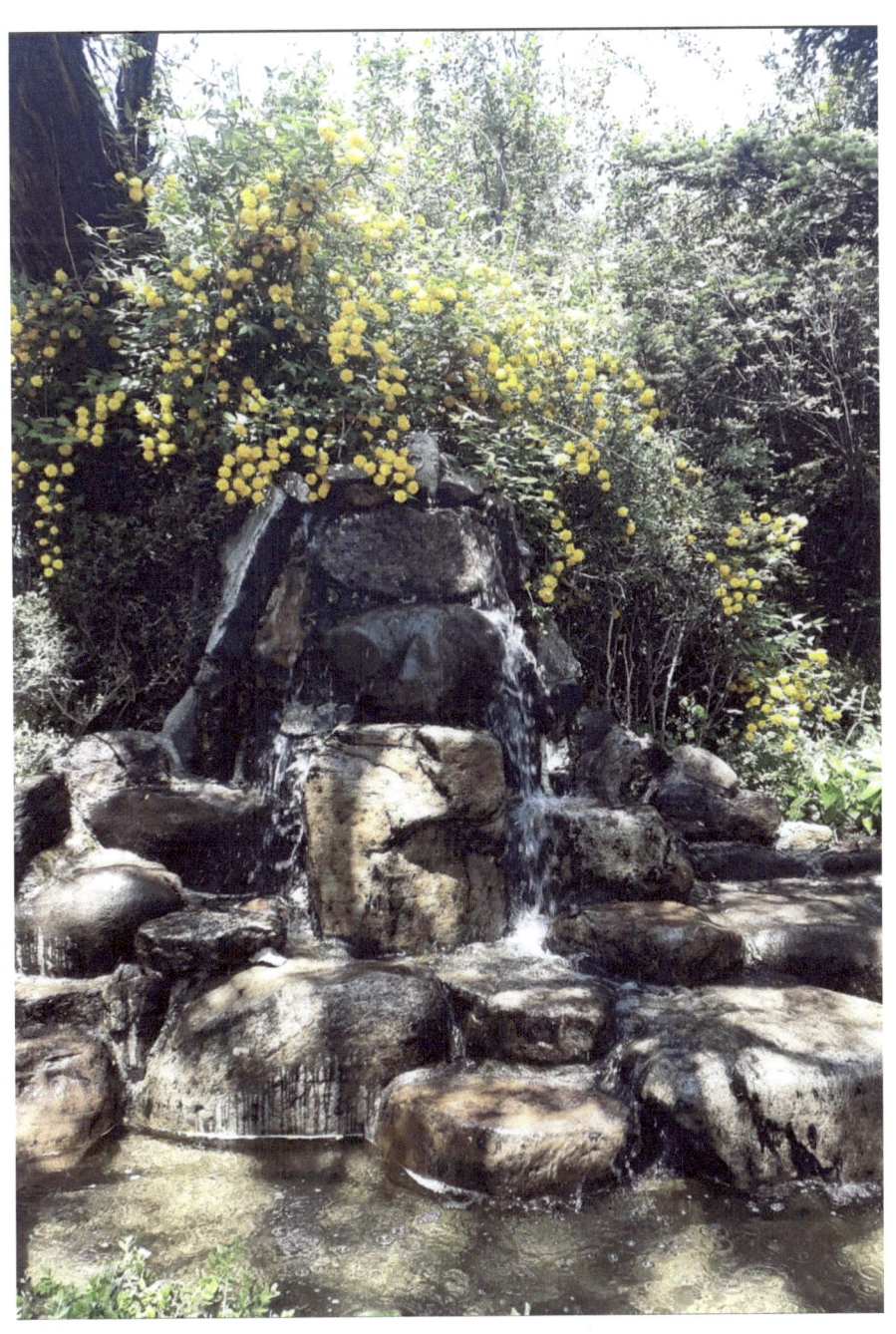

THE WHOLE WORLD HAD CALLED HER HEARTLESS.
YET THE FLOWERS BELIEVED OTHERWISE.

HORIZON SPEAKS

Ever since moving away from the land of steppes, I've looked and looked for a clean slate of horizon. There was none to be found. There were either buildings or mountains that crowded and clogged my desperate view. I lamented: will I ever see a wide strip of land again?

Then the ocean found me, laughing at my stupidity and calling me a narrow-minded blockhead. Well!

Let me jump in to see how open-minded YOU can be.

Someday, if I ever learn to swim...

CREAMY BLUE, AND NOT AS ICY AS IT LOOKS.

SUMMER HAIKU

Close your eyes, feel it,
Some things are better that way -
You dazzling sunlight

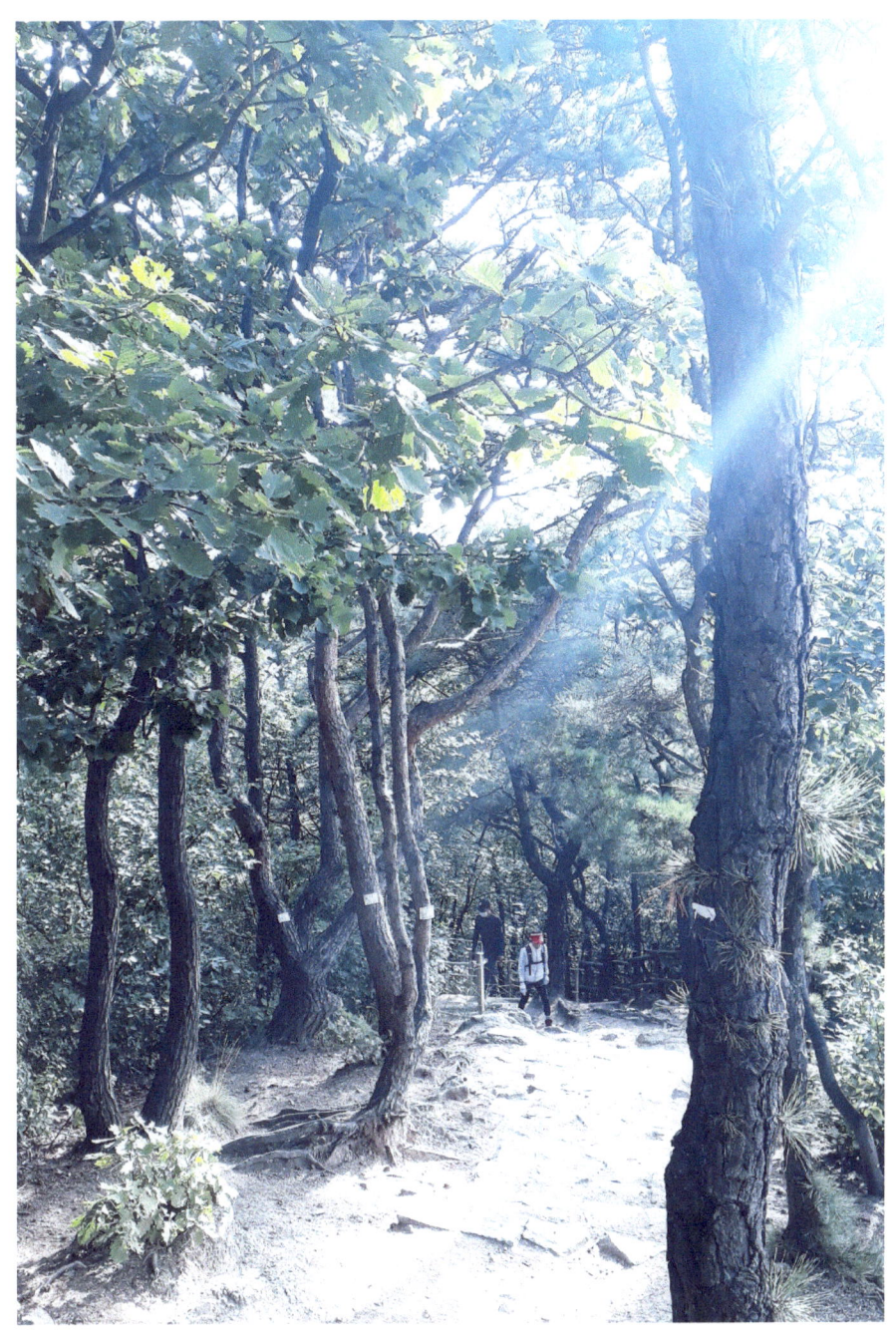

GRASP BEYOND THE VISIBLE.

A CRY OF A DRAGONFLY

As we neared the rocky peak,
Guess who got there before us?

Veni, Vidi, Vici!

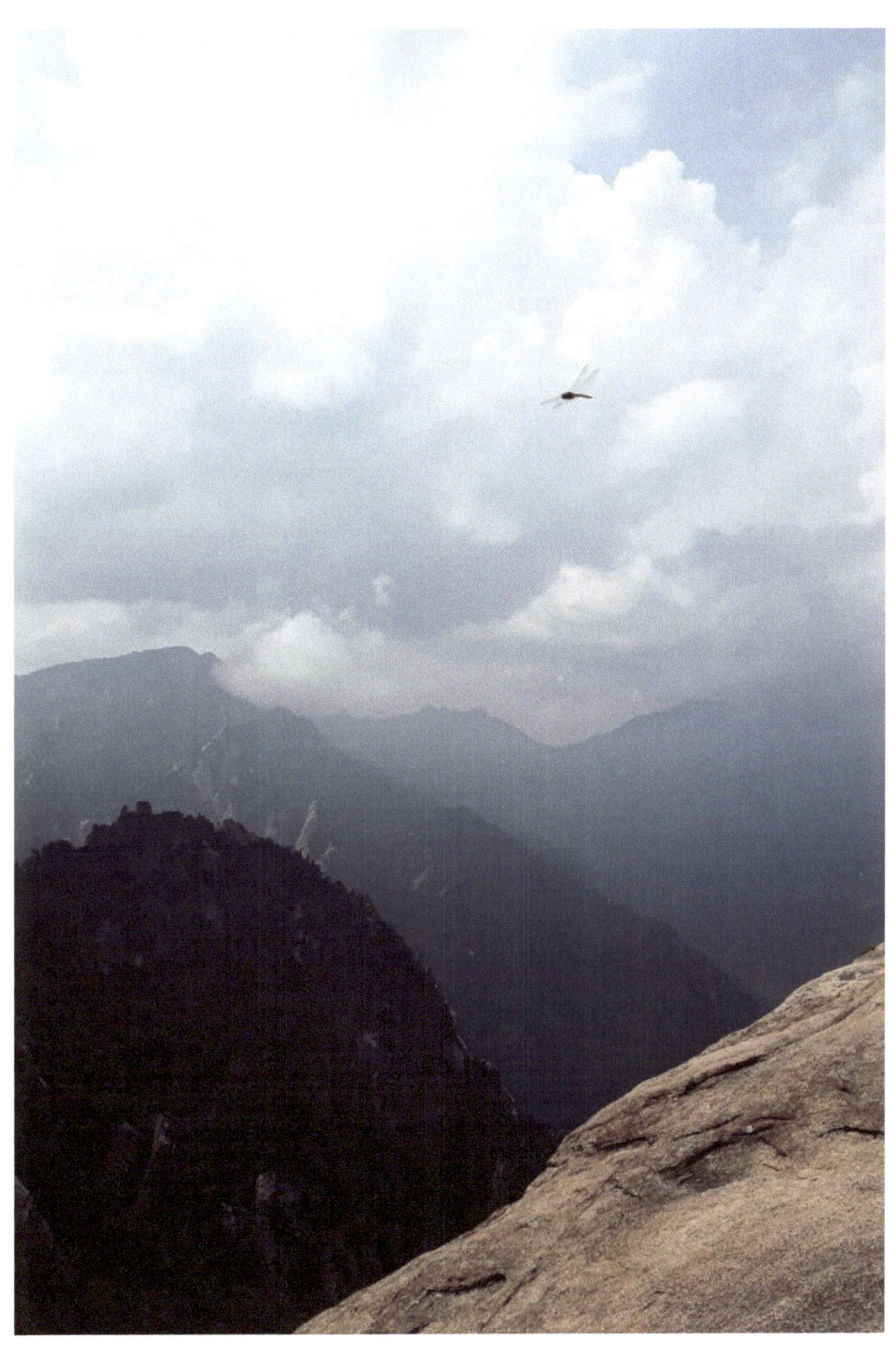

I LET HIM ROAR HIS VICTORY OVER ME.

FROM SOLE TO DEEP

Lassie in the restless deep,
Come pouncing, crashing over me;
Fear not of thrashing nightmares,
Imprint on me with your teary sole -
Destiny spelled eternity

Rend the ocean, dig out treasures -
Dearest memories buried deep,
Then shall we trample tides of death
Till all that remains are dewdrops,
Vaporing under dancing sole

Till dawn awakes, but you shall dream
And rest upon my solid gold,
Till you hear my beating sole
Beating, beating off the dark
That paved your way to me - that restless deep

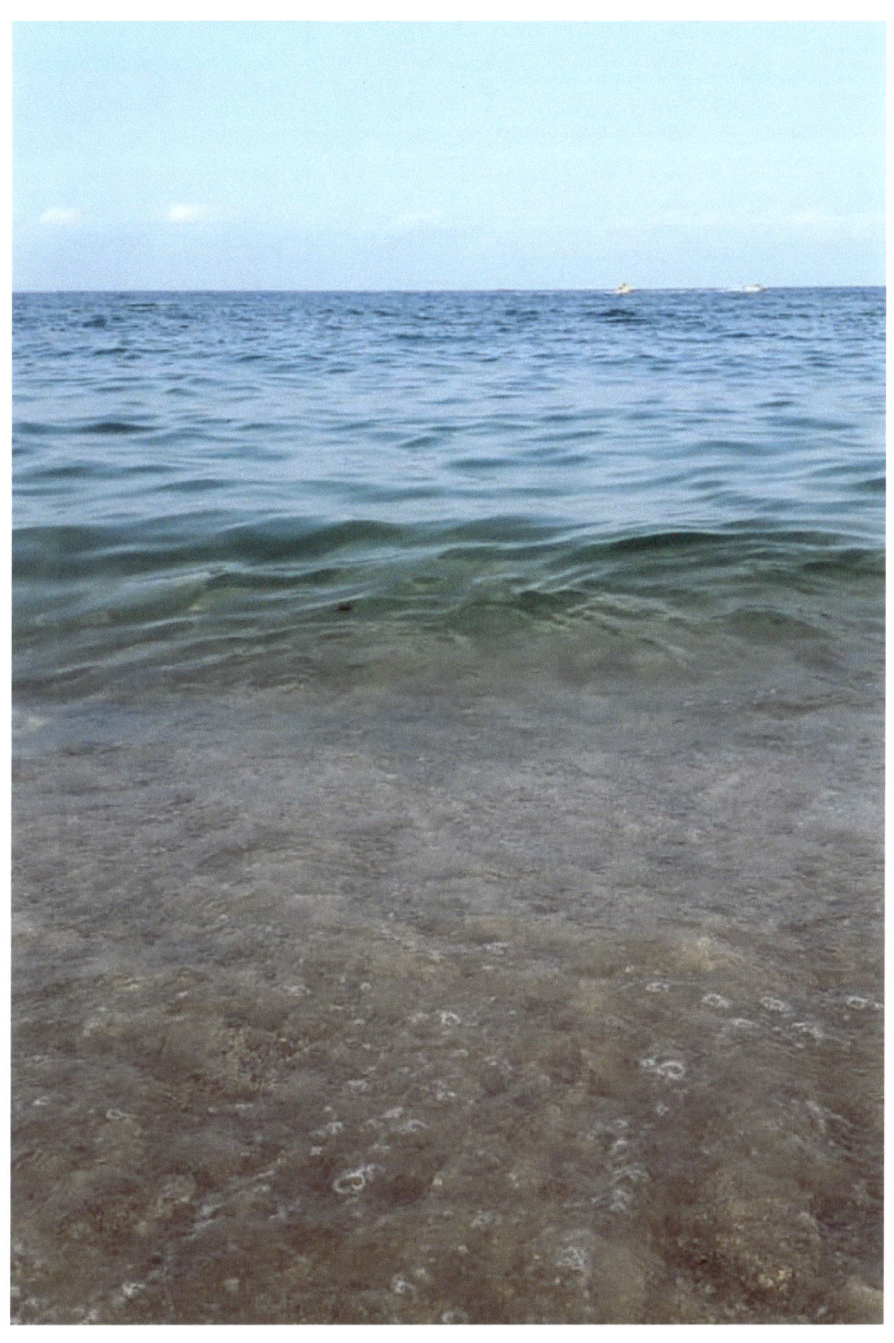

THE SANDY SHORE WAS HER SOLE COMFORTER.

UMMA

She had nothing to lose.
So she spread her wings and sang to the trees.

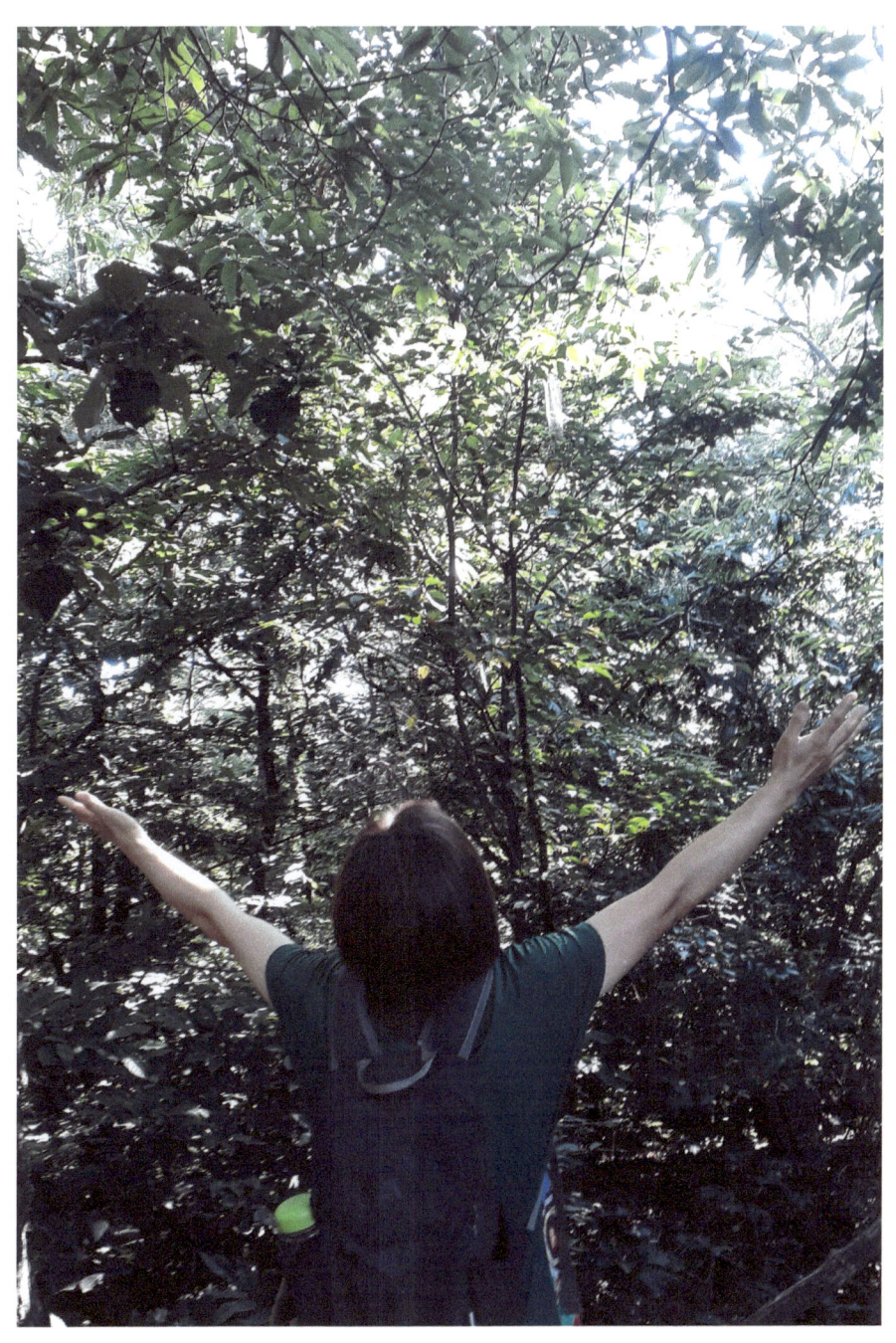

A MOTHER OF TEN.

FRIENDS FOREVER

Assuredly we were friends before birth -
This angel to call mine.
We'd soared the purple skies,
And taunted the gathering darkness.

When my fate was sealed for good,
She'd volunteered to come down first
To protect me from the world,
To love and rear me as her own.

She thinks I'm crazy -
I don't care.
She had forgotten,
I have remembered.

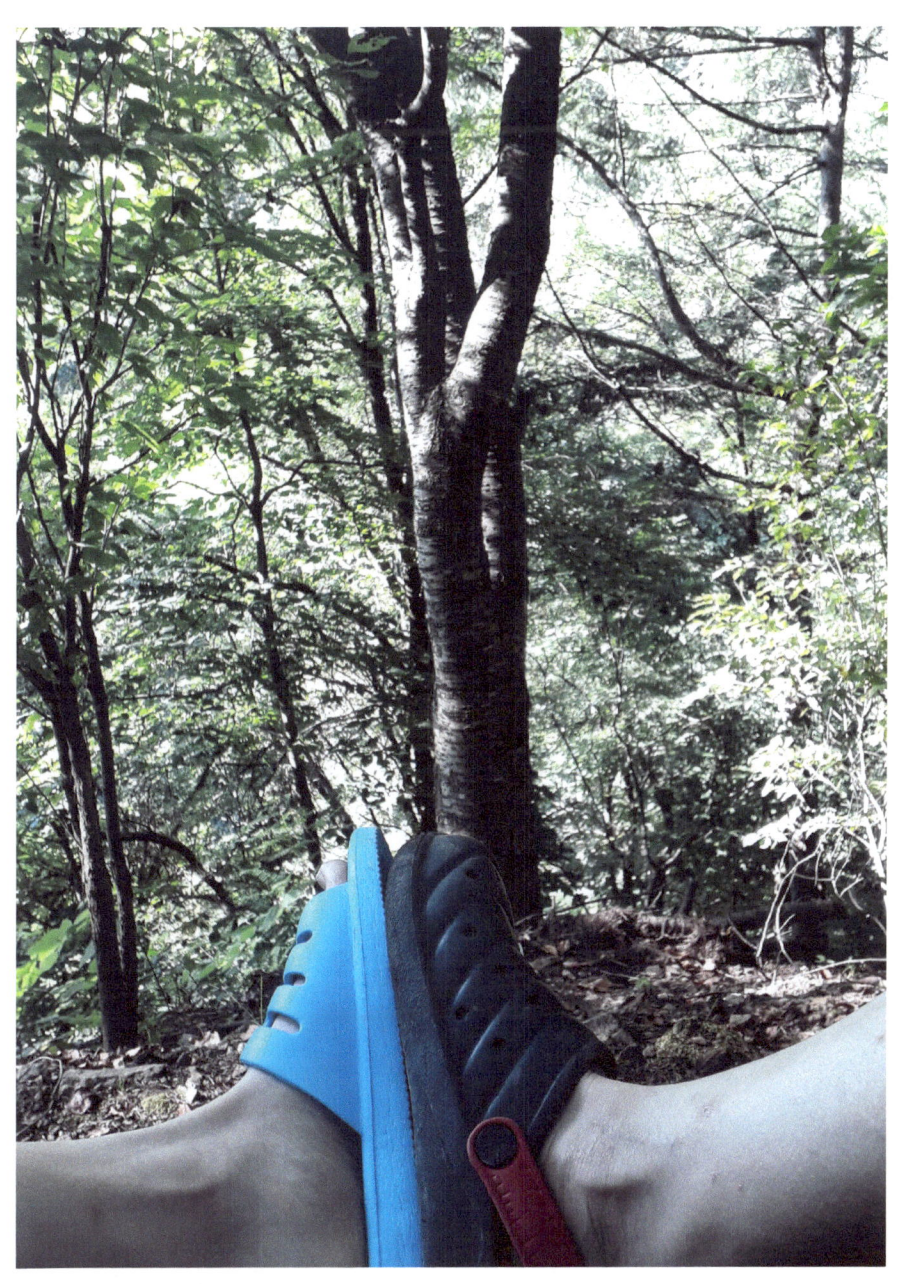

IMPOSSIBLY PERFECT - FRIENDS.

INFINITE PEACE

Time can be stopped.
Just hear the currents ripple.

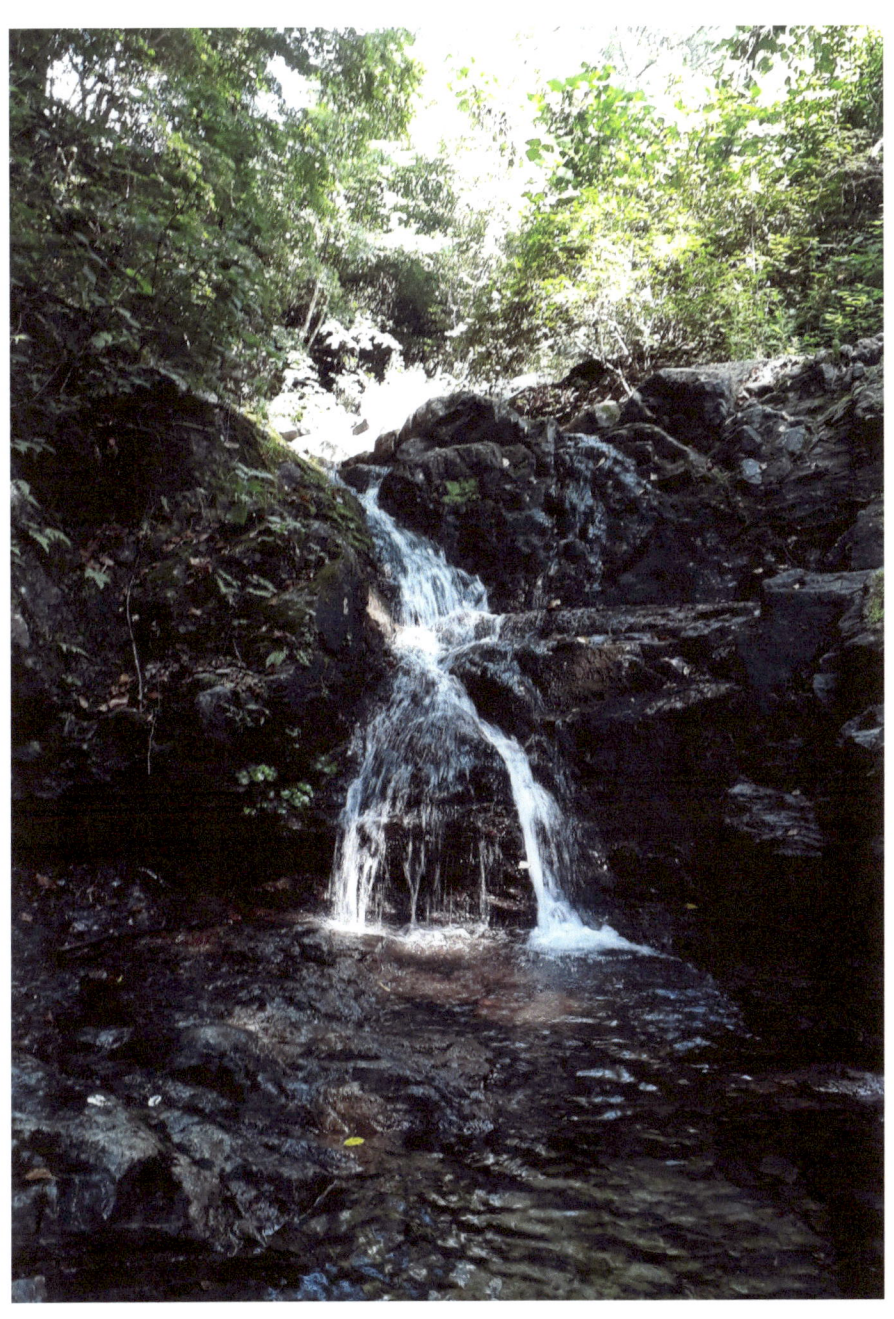

IN THAT NAMELESS VALLEY WHERE CURRENTS OF TIME BECAME RIPPLES OF PEACE.

SWEET PRESENCE

He is up there.
And with us down here.

Basking in His presence is
The ultimate joy and honor of mankind.

Breathe.
And let His pleasure seep into your soul.

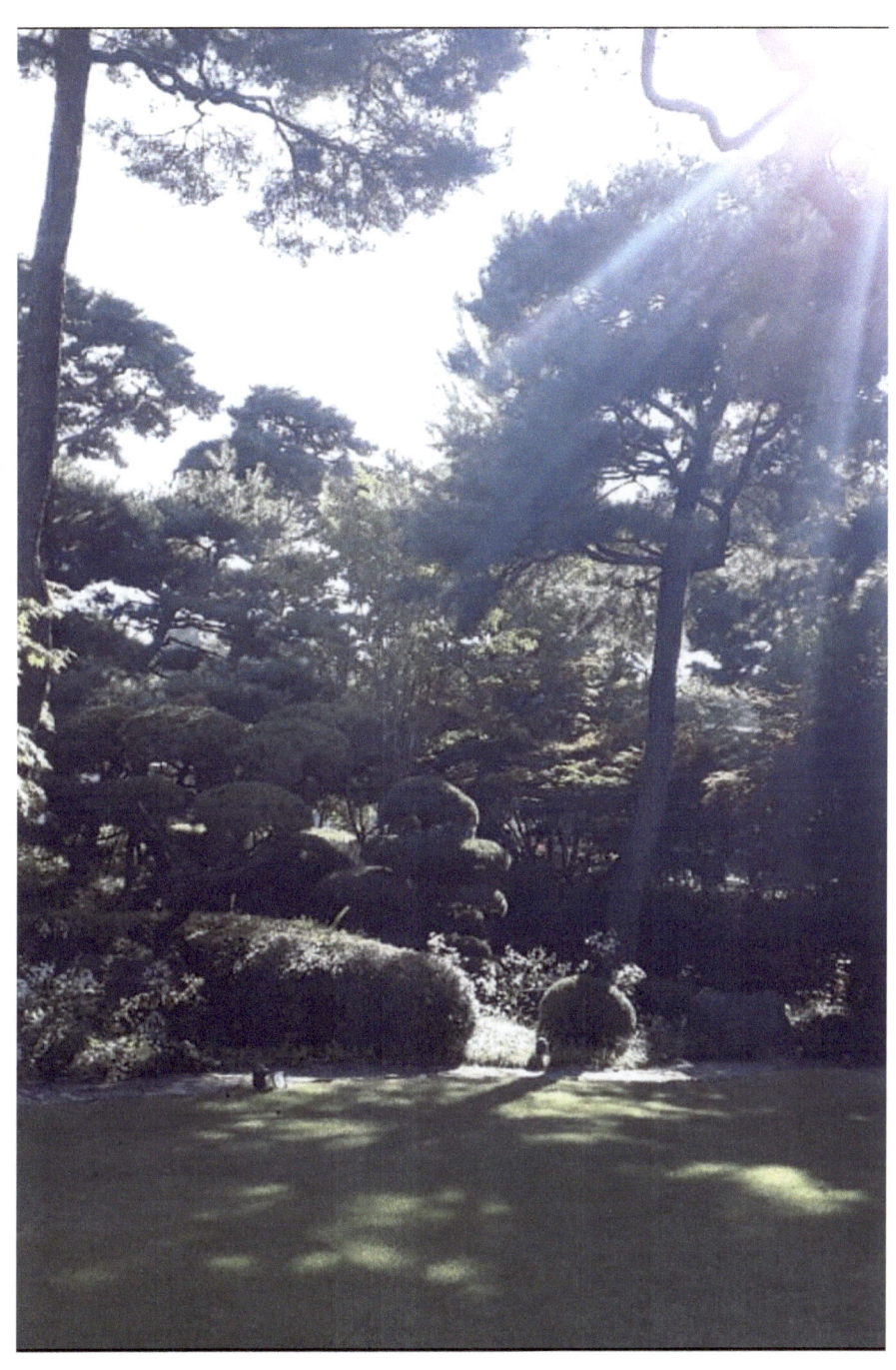

COME INTO THE GARDEN. ALONE.

ILIAD & BEAUTYBERRY

I cannot say I love your story, Homer.
I cannot say I enjoy your book as much
as I love the Lord of the Rings.
No, quite the contrary.

You are boring, you are frivolous.
You are brutal and annoying.

So here's a beautyberry for you, dear,
before being escorted back
to the top of the bookshelf.

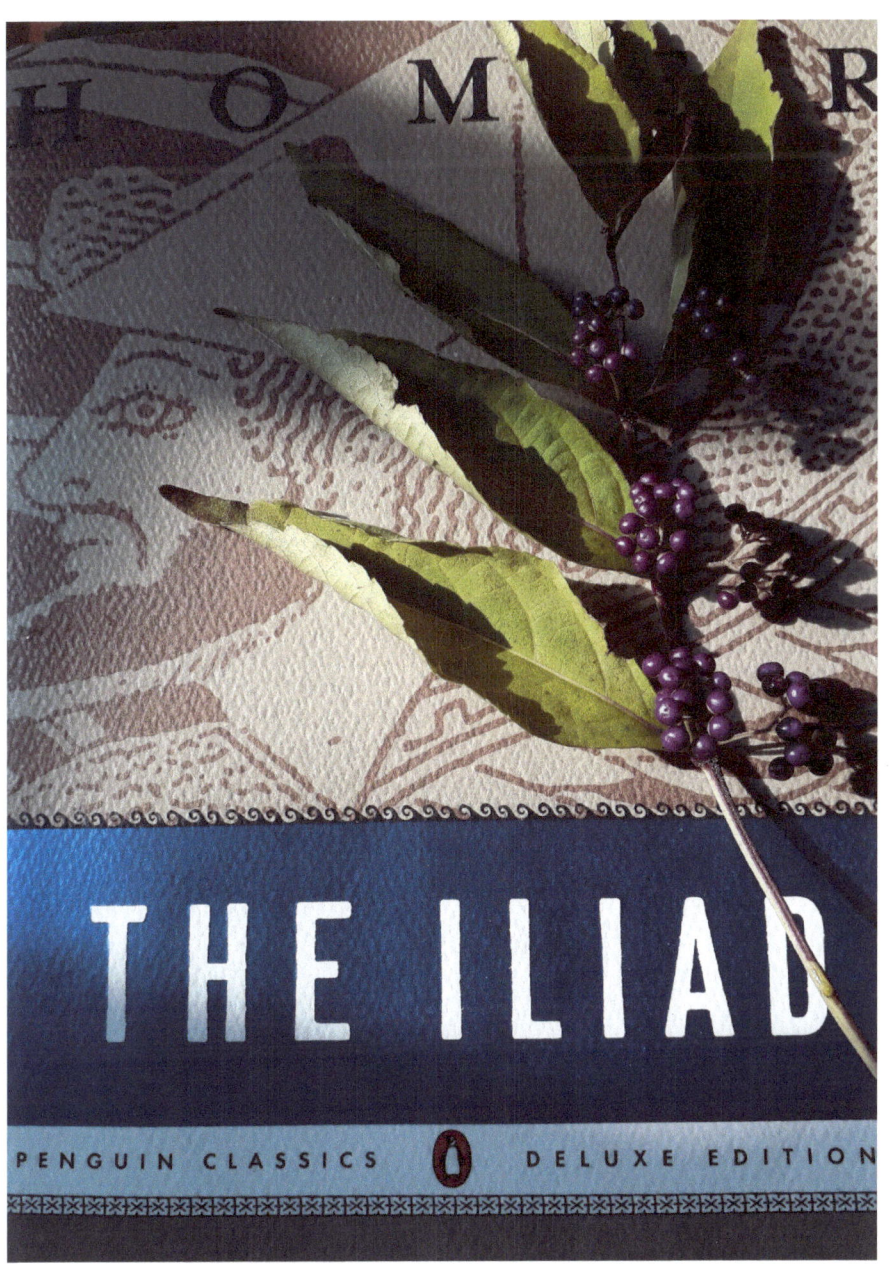

LET THAT BE A TOAST TO EVERYTHING I DON'T SEE THE
GOOD OF, YET IS MADLY PRAISED BY THE WORLD.

AUTUMN HAIKU

Shatter to display

As long as the earth endures

Dashing, child of dawn

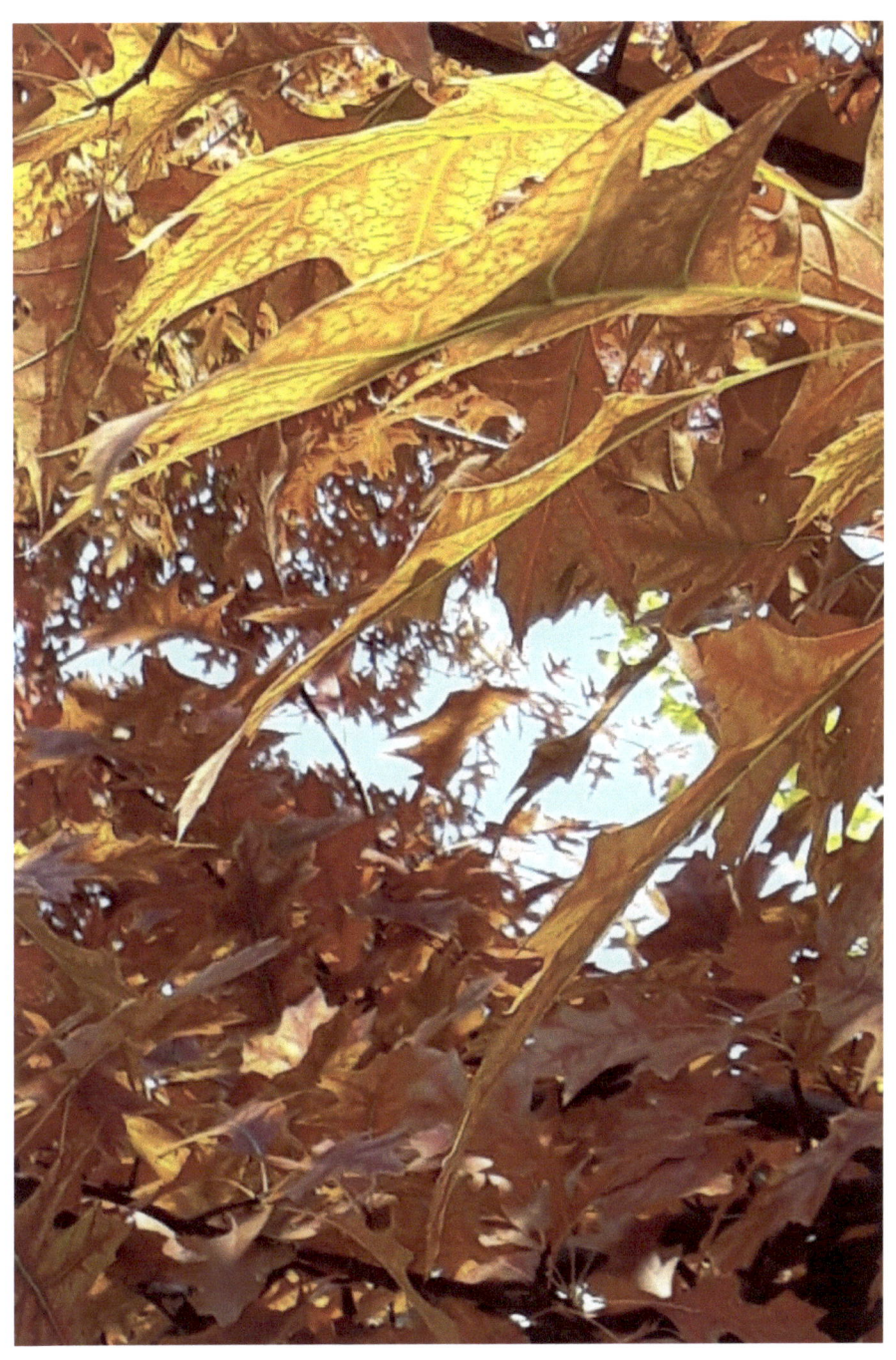

AUTUMN SWIRLS.

MUTUAL HEALING

We all need that quiet space,
that alone time with nature
Where all noises in our heads,
both carnal and pious,
Are shushed to an awe.

It was a liberating moment
When the ocean helped me find my voice
And I in turn his.

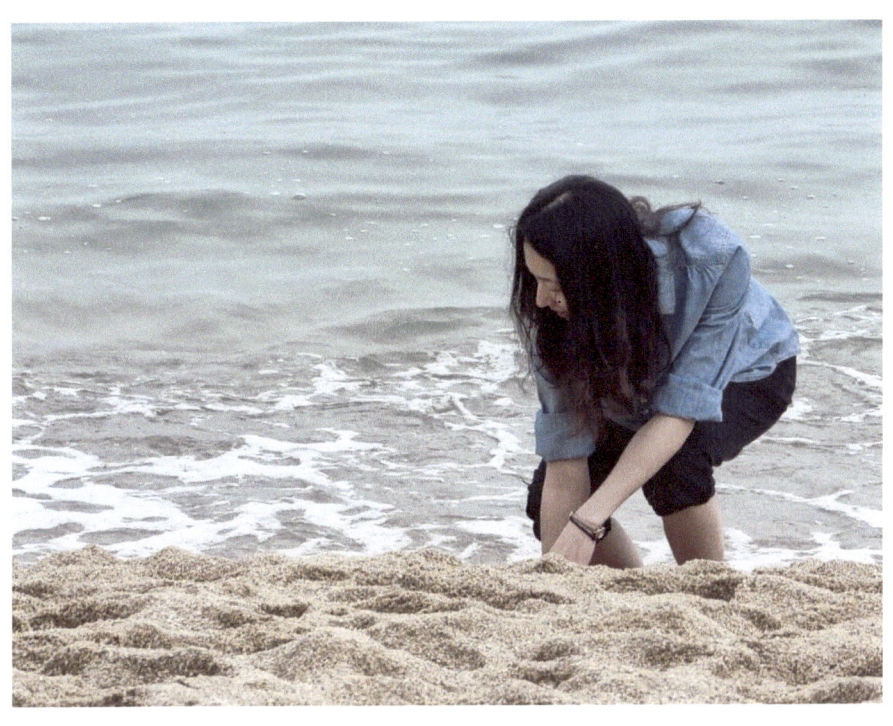

COAXED UNTIL THEY SPOKE TO ME. FIRST A ROAR, NEXT A LAUGHTER, THEN A SILENT CRY.

SHOOTING STARS

You may never see a shooting star.
You may never own a shooting star.
No matter, dear one.

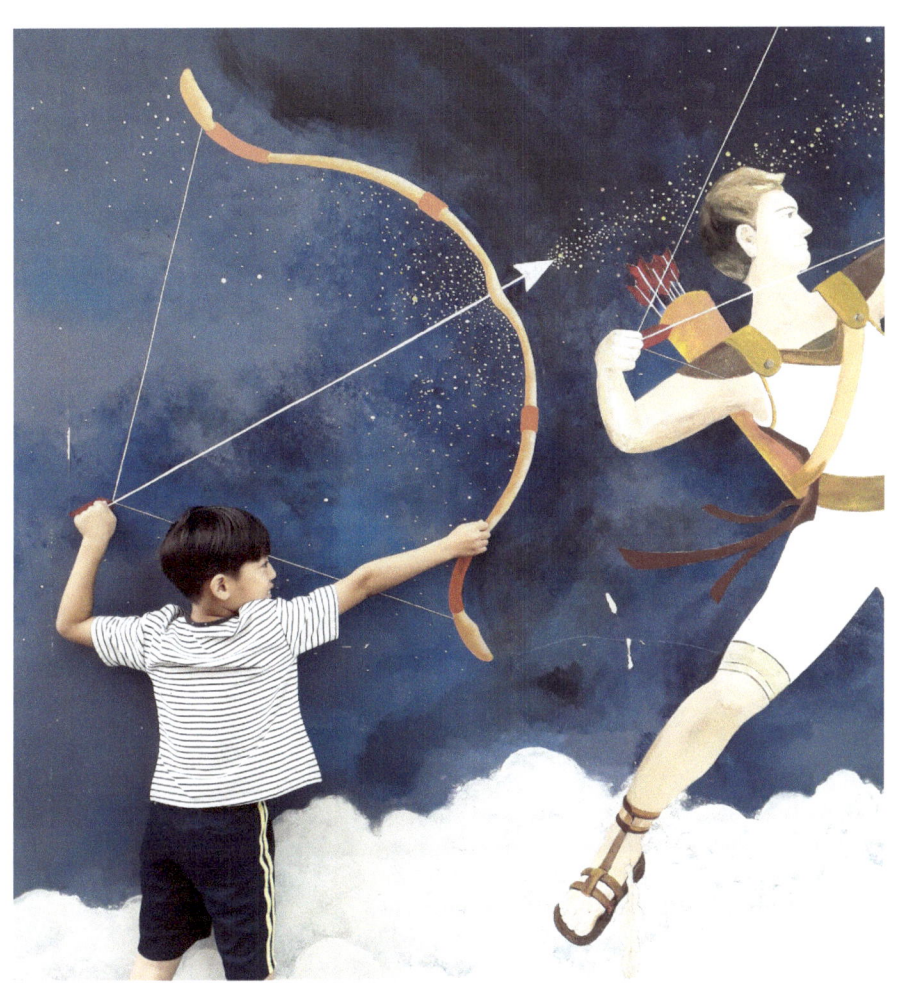

JUST GO SHOOT ONE!

SWING LOW

The yellow little flowers sang vivaciously
as the seasoned leaves fell laughing
into their fold.

"Ah, 'twas a good season!" cry the old.
"A season?" ask the young.
The old do not answer, but happily get ready
to dream.

Hocus. Pocus. Time to focus.

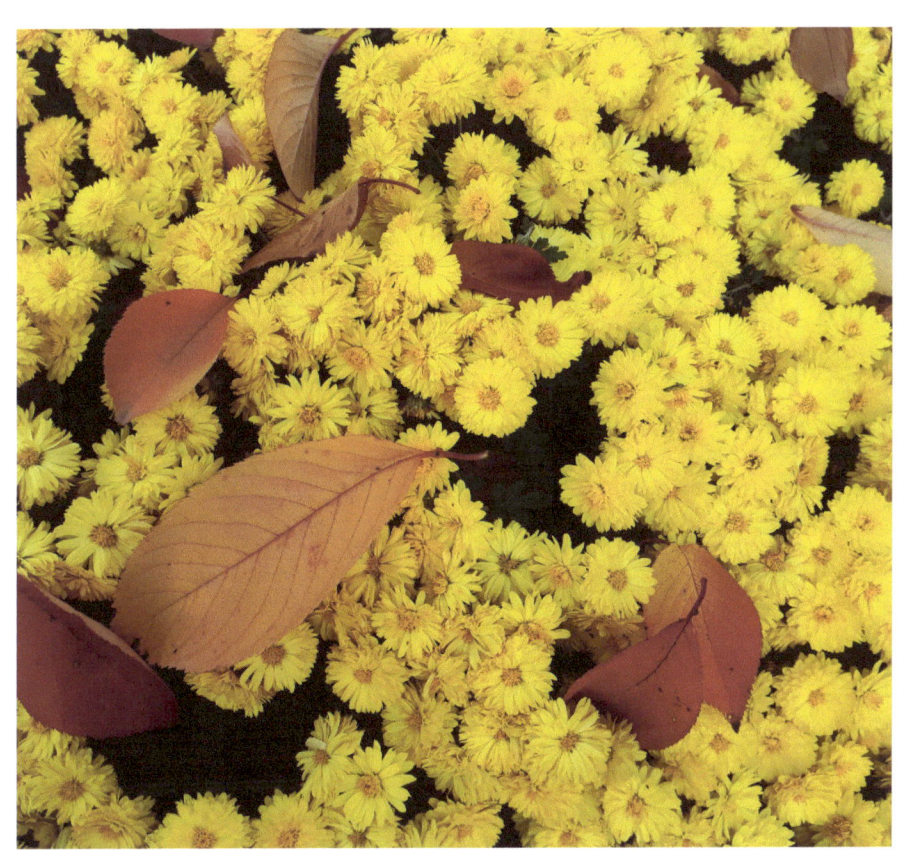

STAY WARM. STAY VALIANT.
COMING FORTH IN AUTUMNY FOAM!

NOSTALGIA

Clutching onto the legacies past,
Declaring on my crumbling faith,
I have writhed to stand - again and again

Was North so ever so harsh, so cold?
Yet yonder have I counted stars
And drew up dreams that no one knew

If days of yearning multiplies
And wind and stars should testify,
The days to visit will come to pass

To give me hope of things unseen,
The starry song once homeland gave -
The wind has catered in tonight

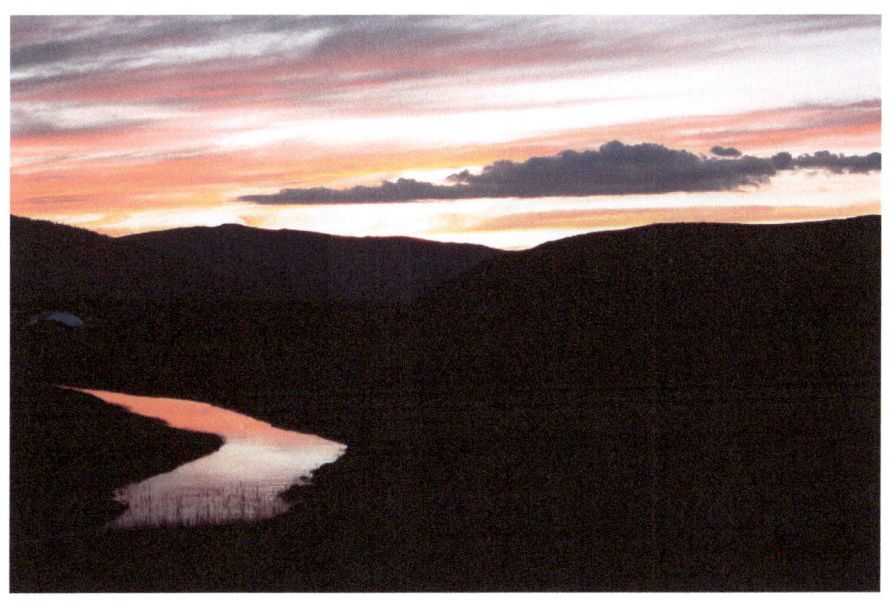

WIND, WIND, BRING ME WHAT IS MINE.

GRANDPA KUHO

You could always see the hilarious side of things.

I wish you had stayed a while longer
and watched me grow to love your humor.

But then, I guess you are doing just that.

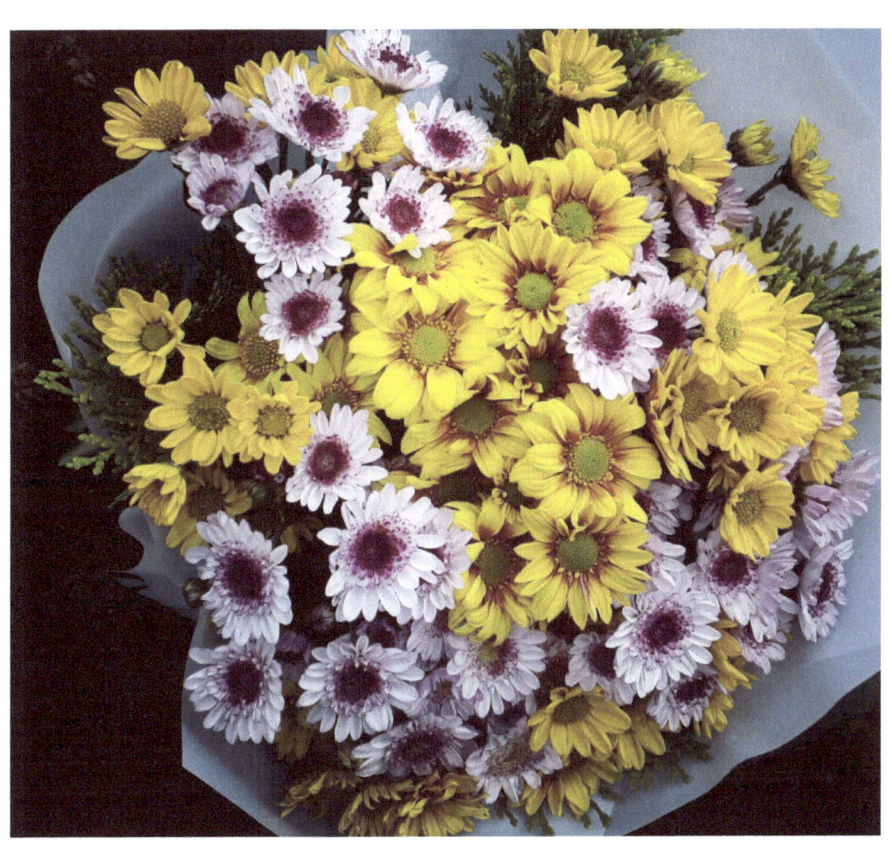

THE YELLOWED MEMORIES WERE BROUGHT TO LIFE
BY THESE LIVELY LITTLE FELLOWS.

STATELY STANDING

My life didn't quite turn out the way I had expected. In some ways, I experienced so much breakthrough that was beyond my expectation - like finally learning to get up early! And in some ways, I battled emotional and mental pain that was way past my imagination.

Yet through it all, I am still standing. Standing stately in a gown of - of drabness. Someday, perhaps, I could put on a gown of gaiety like these dancing autumn leaves and be comfortable in them, but not now. And that is OK.

I am thankful to be where I am. Thankful to be standing, living and breathing.

In my humblest opinion, to live is to win!

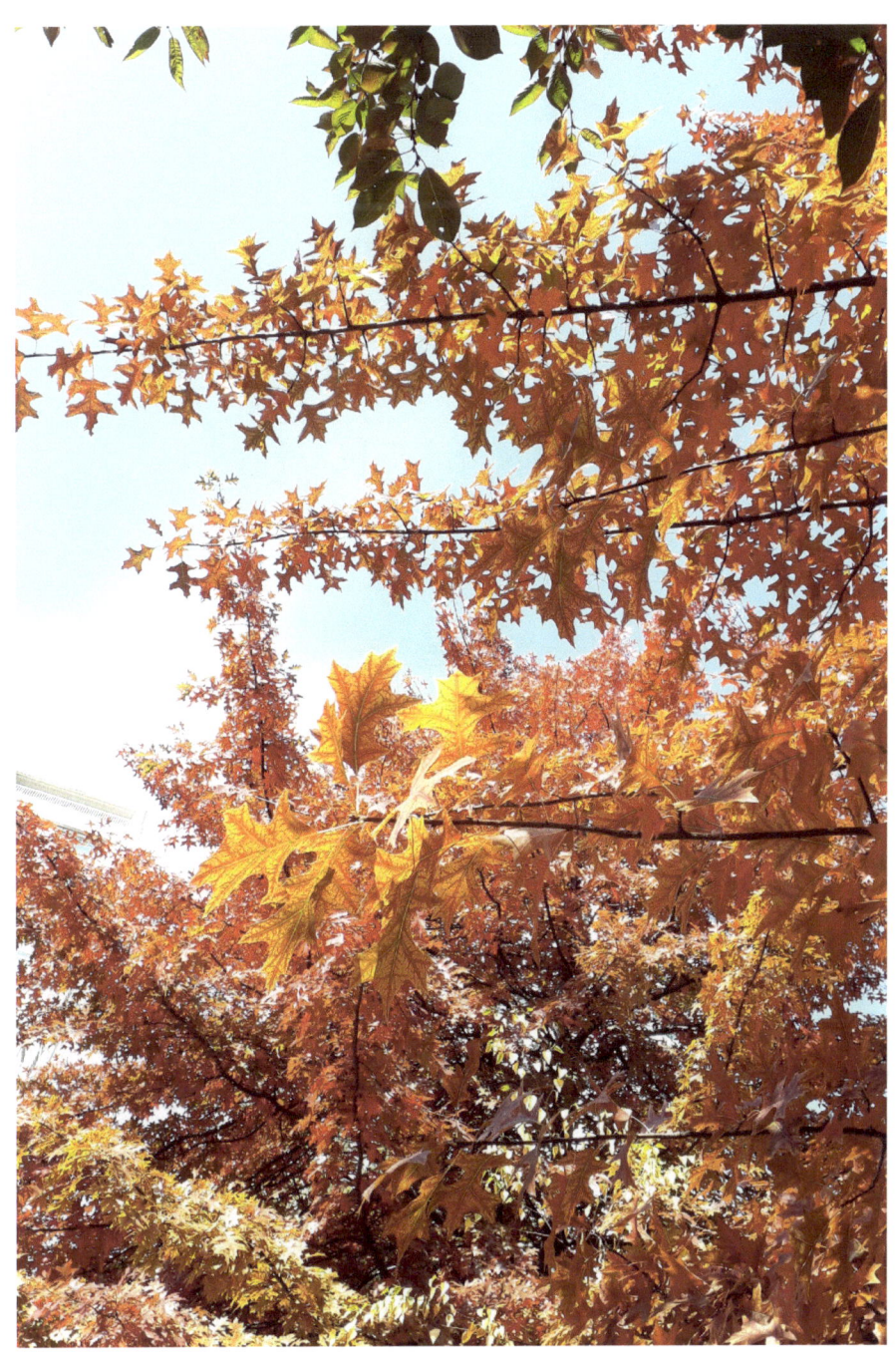

IN A GOWN OF GAIETY.

PEPPER HARVEST

Mostly they were good, but sadly,
some had to be thrown away –
they were beyond repair.

This is the artwork they painted
before the final departure.

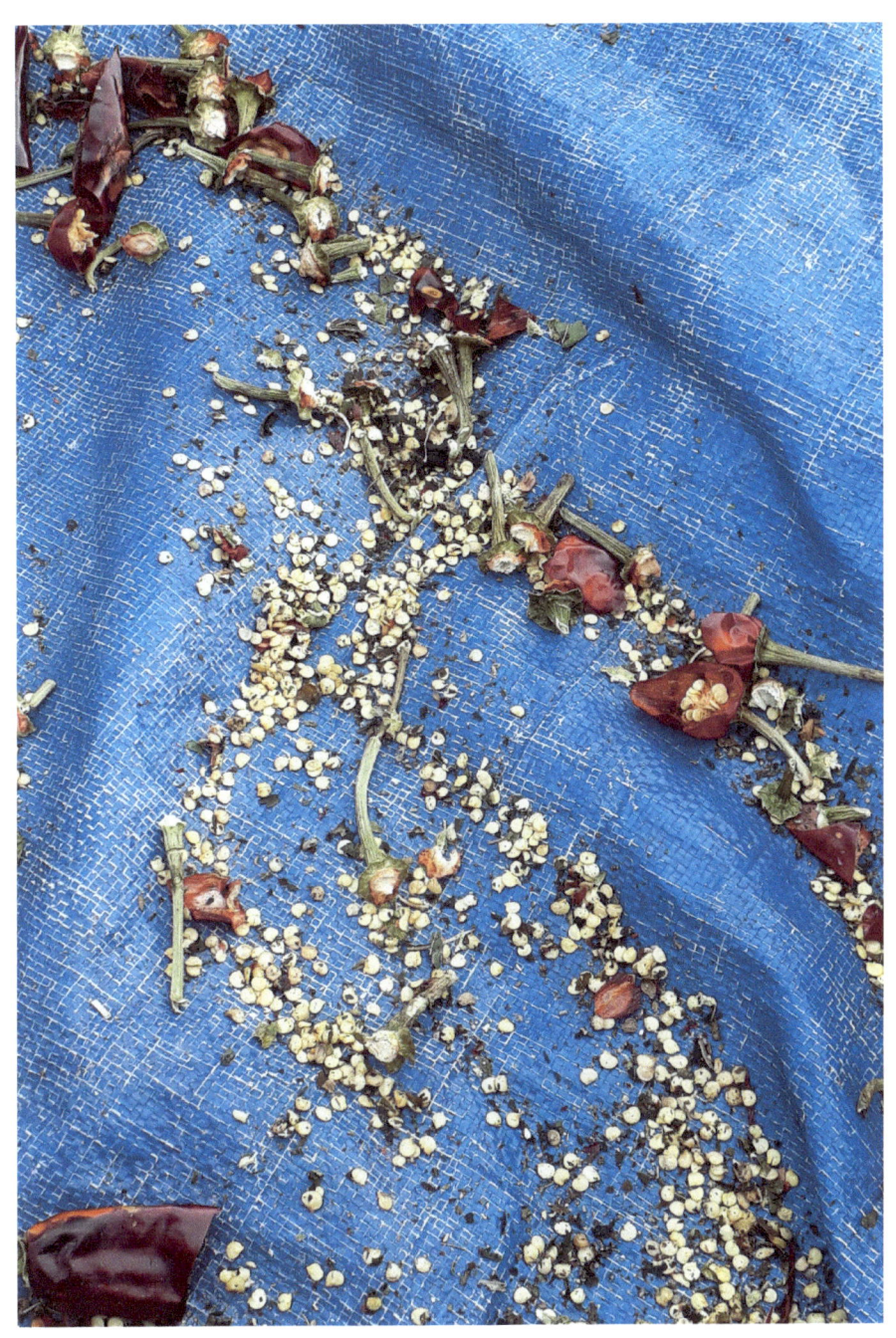

WHEN THE ROLL WAS CALLED UP YONDER.

WINTER HAIKU

Merrily Christmas!
'Tis the joy of aging, folks,
You're the Santa now!

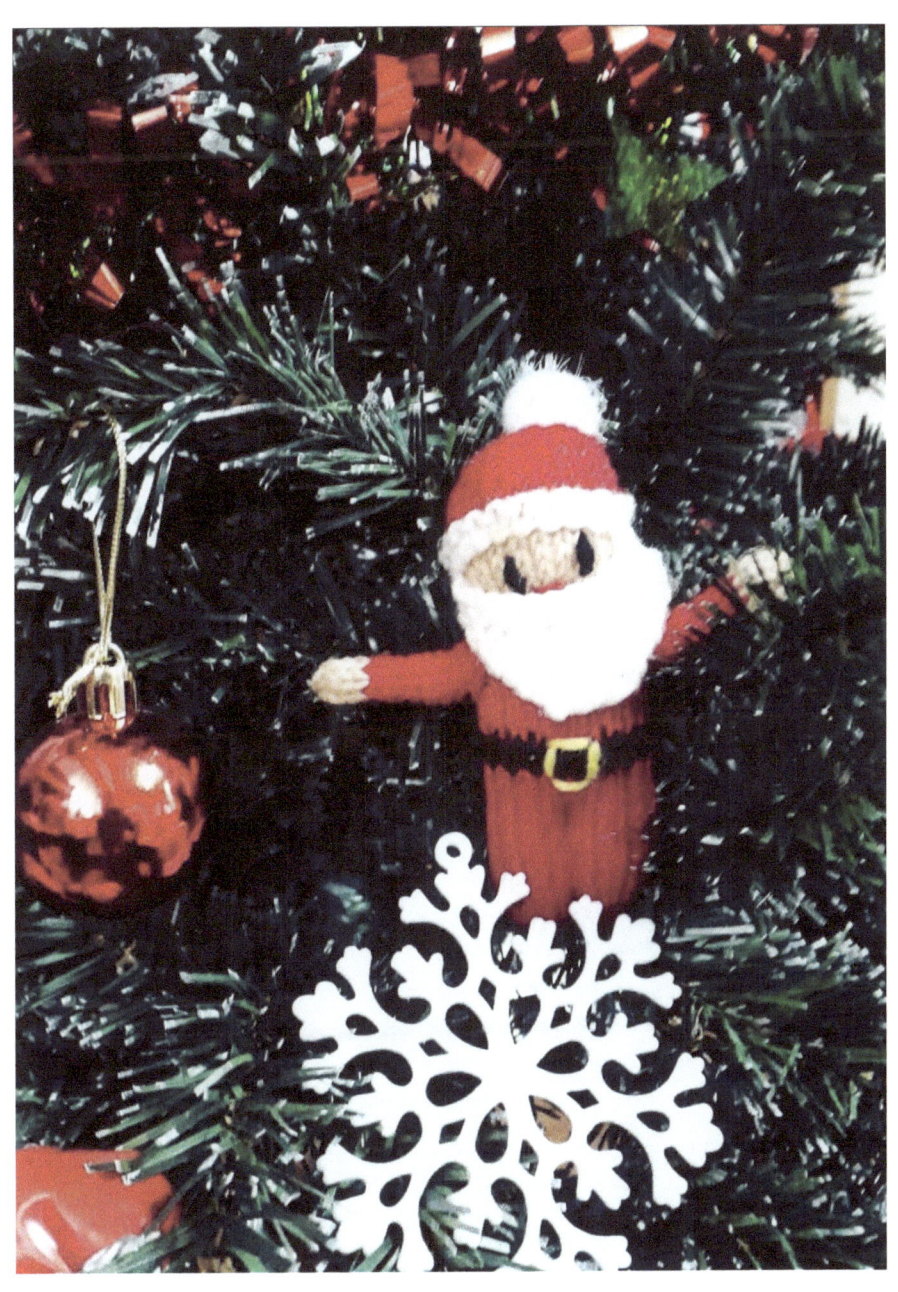

IT'S TIME TO MAKE MEMORIES FOR THE BUBBLY ONES!

FIREWORKS

The truth shall set you free.

It did, breaking off all ties to let me fall
untethered to the unknown.

Fell, fell - to what felt like an endless darkness.
Then found myself flapping and weeping,
And again, weeping and flapping.

I had wings.

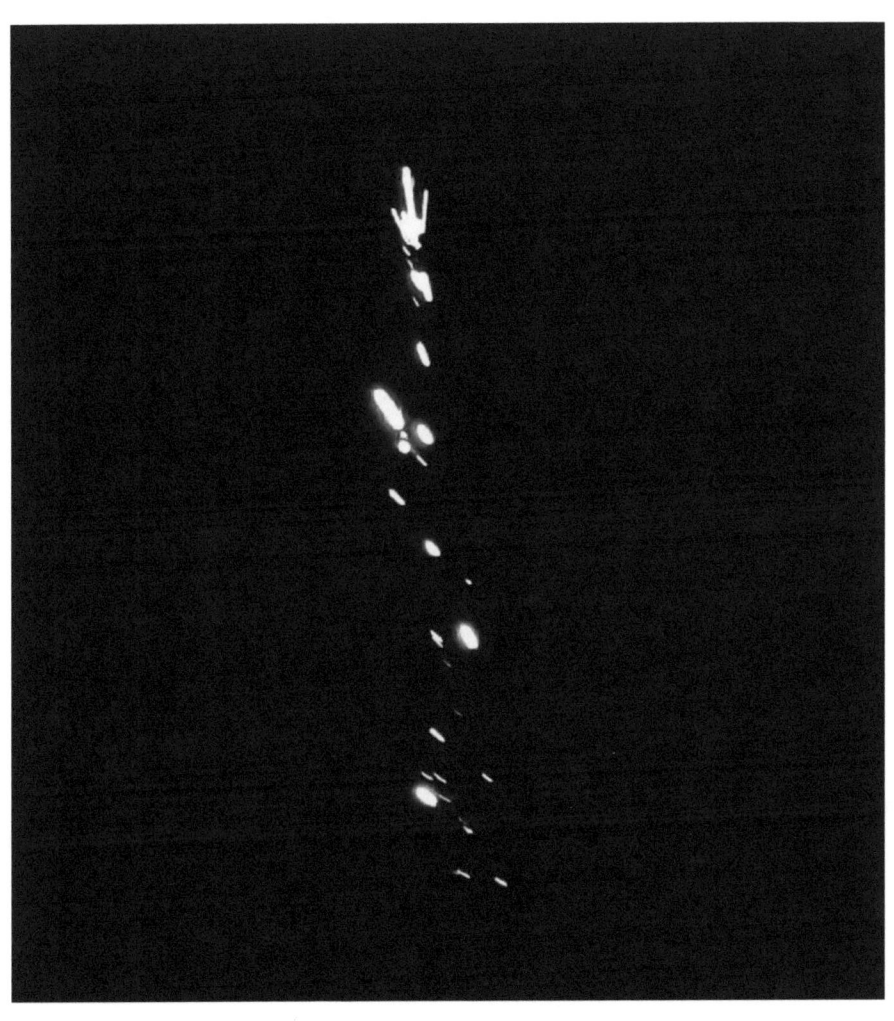

THERE IS BITTERNESS THAT DISCOVERS YOUR DESTINY.

TRUE SATISFACTION

You said you've forgotten my past
You said I'm unique in your eyes
It's hard to agree when all I see
Is shame, dust and ashes

Look deep into my eyes
My clouded eyes
Till I know that I am yours
And you are mine, mine alone

Stretching out my hands to meet
That yonder cloud-melting sky -
Peace alone satisfies
In your fiery eyes

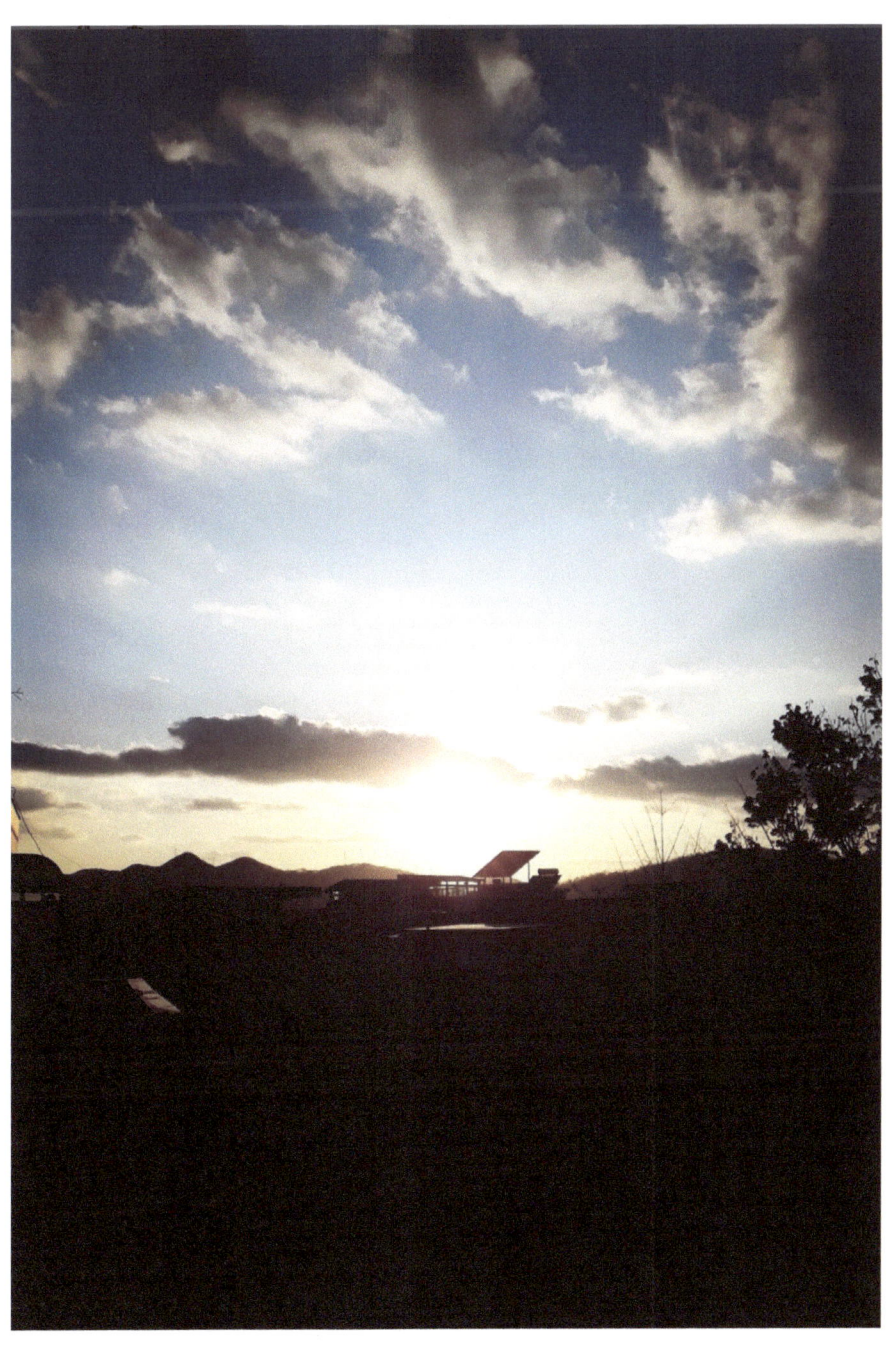

THE ACHES AND CRACKS WERE CONSUMED IN GLORY.

THAT WILDISH STREAK

Pepper's got to dream in day time,
Or the night air will bog her down.

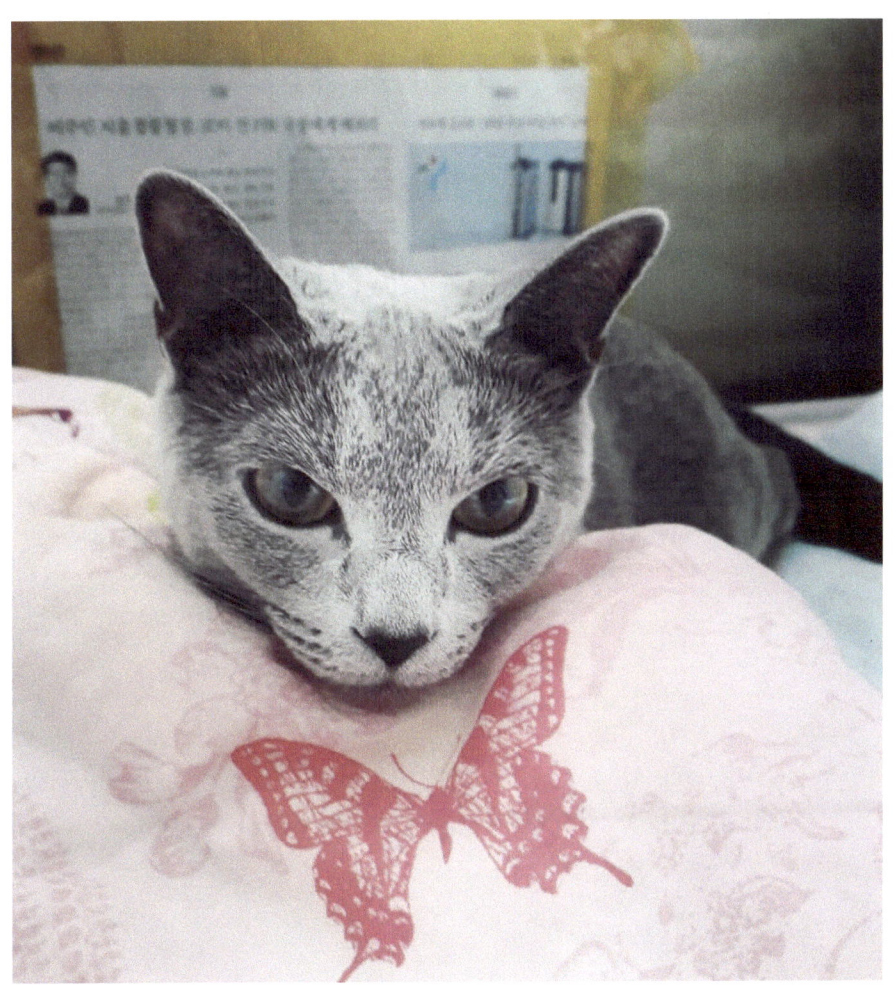

POUNCE!

WHERE VICTORY LIES

Glow, glow, do not fuddle

Ever stable in a muddle

Brightly? Oof, just stand your ground

Flicker, ever yonder flicker

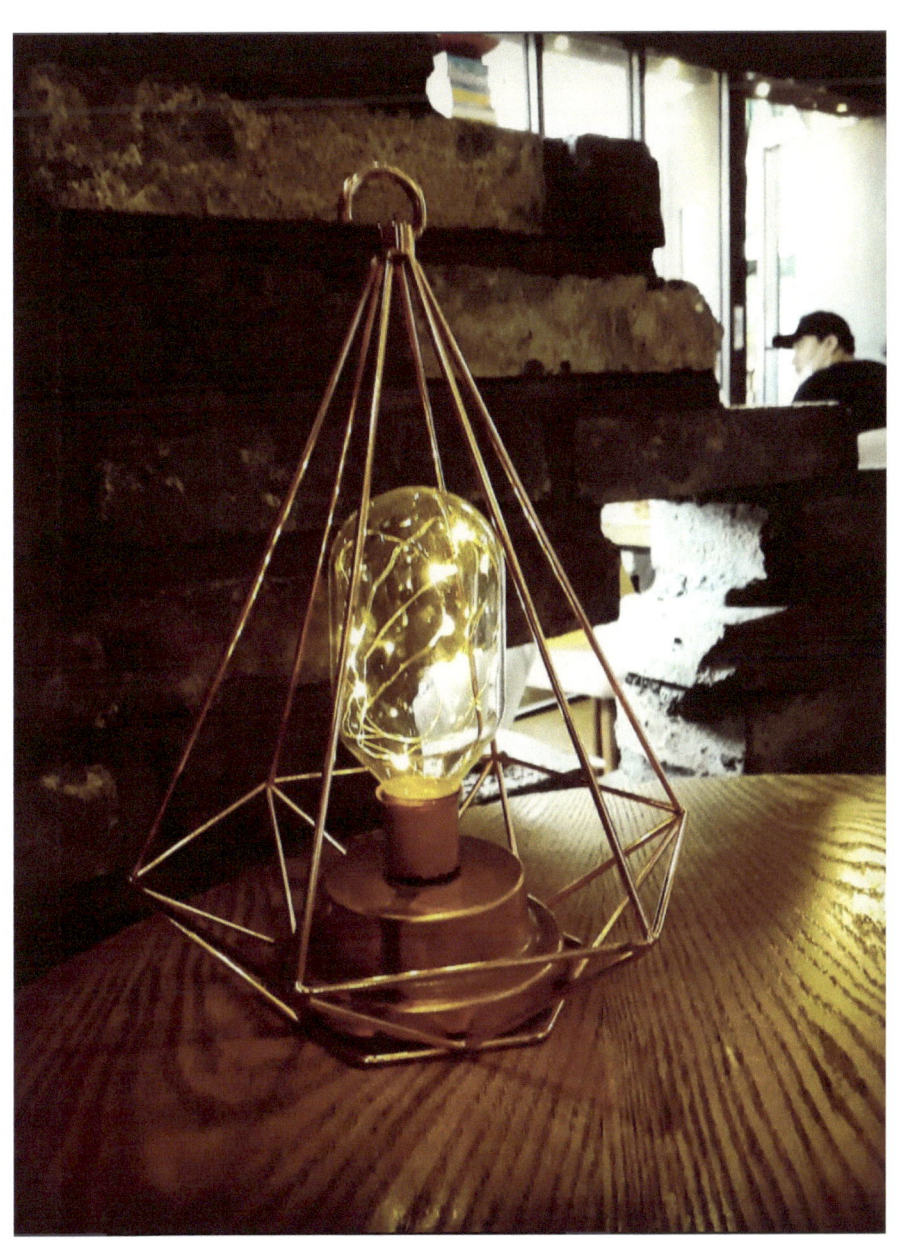

STAND, STAND - THAT'S THE KEY!

DAISY, DAISY

You used to stay for a single summer
Wild and free under purple skies,
Your yellow eyes would sing to me
And twinkle in the night

Stay awhile, awhile with me
For awhile can be a short long while;
Daisy, Daisy, loyal kind -
Come and seal my memories tight

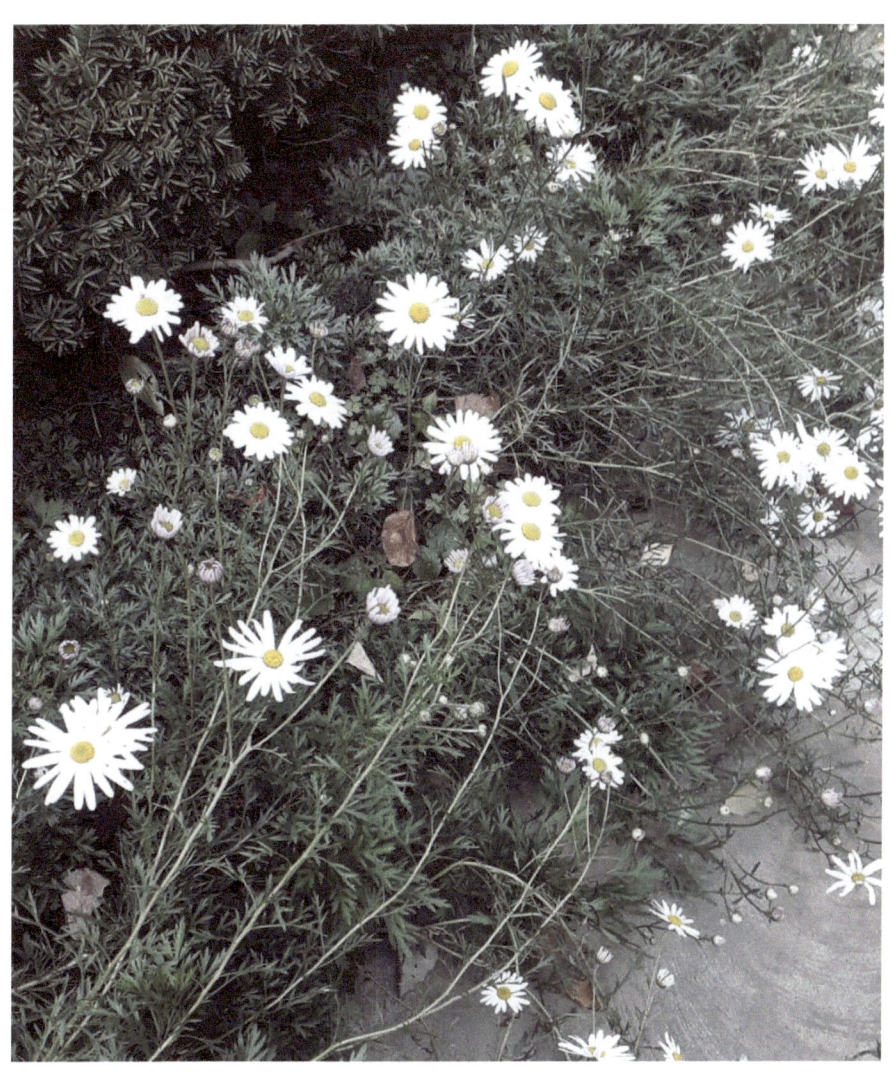

THE PAST IS TO LET GO, BUT NEVER THE MEMORIES.

MORE THAN A CONQUEROR

She had conquered cancer.
And many other things that I couldn't fathom.
Yet she was ready for more - for life.

There was something resilient about the food that she served and the tears that she shed while her life was remembered. Life that was tragic, miraculous and insanely beautiful.

That morning I gave up my no-flour diet and ate everything on the table: from pasta to sweet macarons. The side effects that I had feared did not occur that day. Nor after.

To this day, I am eating my pasta and pastries. Side effects-free. Healed.

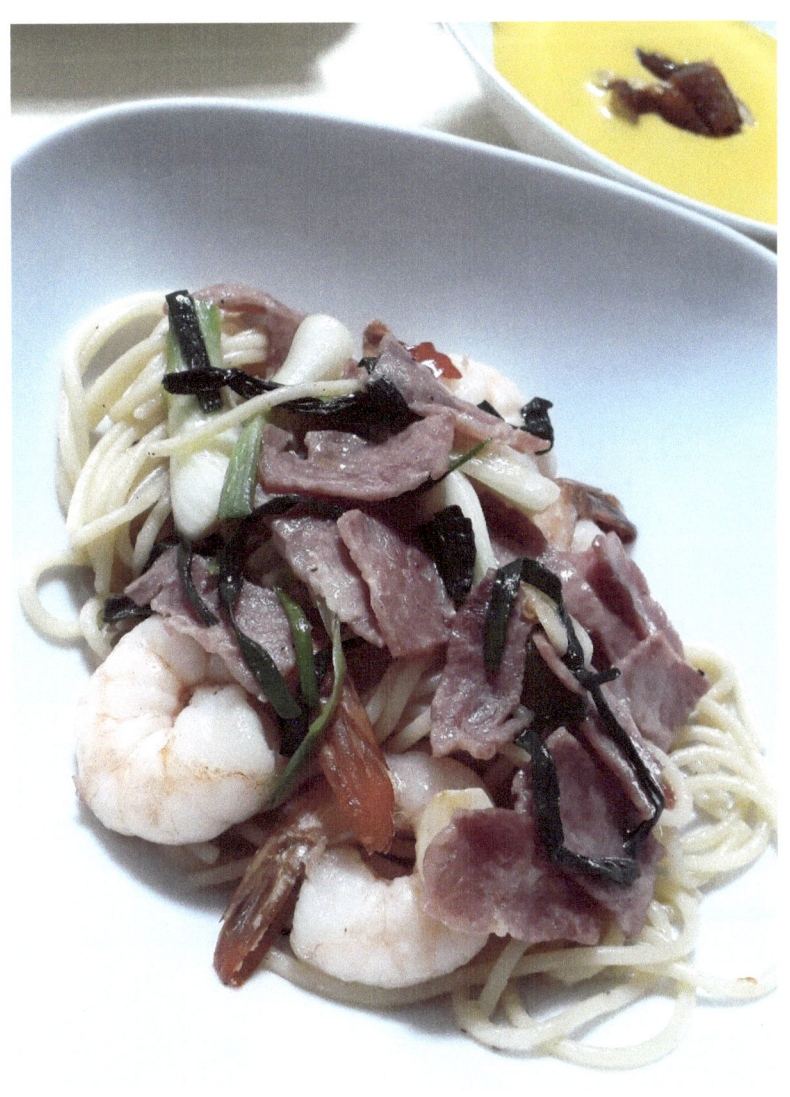

CHEF SUSANNA'S MIRACLE PASTA.

SOLID FRIENDS

Solid friends are what you glean
And cherish in your aching palms,
Sloppy friends are what you're given
In a box that oft explodes

Keep a list, update it now,
Memories sweet and incidents sour;
Sift it with a bit of wisdom
Dust it with a stroke of grace

Surely you must know who would
Regard YOU as their solid friend,
Send your greetings now and then
And make that old bond precious

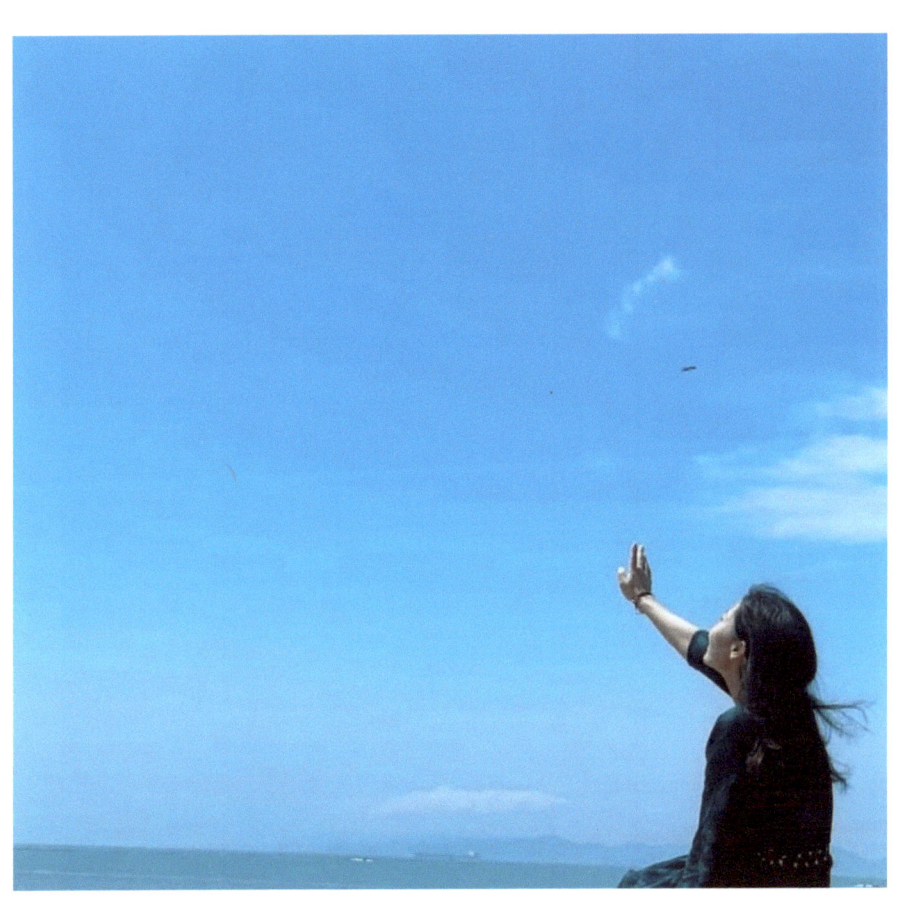

DESTINY WILL BRING YOU FRIENDS,
BUT IT IS YOUR JOB TO CHERISH THEM.

ABOUT THE AUTHOR

As a child,
she went tiger hunting with her Grandfather.
Invisible ones, of course.

As a teenager,
she befriended a raven,
using her superpower - telepathy.

As an adult,
she hollered enough
and shared her thoughts with the world.

www.ingramcontent.com/pod-product-compliance
Lightning Source LLC
Chambersburg PA
CBHW040320220526
45473CB00009B/2504